826 BOOKS

826CHI
www.826chi.org

All proceeds from the sale of this book directly benefit
free student programming at 826CHI.

ISBN: 978-1-934750-25-4

Cover by Aaron Renier with lettering by Thomas Quinn
Interior illustrations by Aaron Renier and Laura Park
Book design by Thomas Quinn

Printed in Canada

826CHI PRESENTS

ANYWHERE
AT ONCE

WRITTEN BY 106 2ND–8TH GRADE STUDENTS

TABLE OF CONTENTS

INTRODUCTION

This is the story of how the story you are about to read came to be. It's the story of how hundreds of students from across the city of Chicago took three characters and brought them to life through a series of epic adventures. It is also the story of the tireless effort of dozens of 826CHI volunteers who crisscrossed the city determined to help these students bring their writing to its fullest potential. The story you are about to read will begin with a boy, a girl, and a lizard, but the story of how that story came to be started on a blustery Friday afternoon at 826CHI.

Coming in from the soon-to-be-colder chill of a Chicago winter, students shook off their coats and joined 826CHI for the start of a two-session workshop that focused on creating a compelling character. Working together in the spirit of true protagonists, this group examined the importance of characters' desires, fears, and secrets, and out of it came a plethora of original heroes ranging from a girl born on a rocket ship to a ghost living in an abandoned pickle jar. (We imagine that ghost is still wandering around somewhere, trailing the scent of brine across the city.) Ultimately, the workshop resulted in the three main characters in the novel you are reading.

And then the action began. Equipped with a set of character traits, an abundance of paper, and a fearless resolve to help third graders sound out "Professor Scalious," 826CHI volunteers spent the next two months working with students in 25 classrooms throughout Chicago. Students were given creative prompts ranging from "Describe your idea of a secret island..." to "Write about Ophelia's first day of school..." Most of the prompts were creative in nature, but some writing was also focused on genres such as poetry, how-to paragraphs, and the persuasive essay, as requested by teachers participating in the project. Writing generated during early visits in the project went on to inspire later prompts such as adventures on Sam's farm and expeditions to outer space. In all, more than 700 students shared their adventures and offered their unique visions of each of the main characters. A complete list of these student contributors is located at the back of this book.

Which led to this story's climax. After an epic review process by 826CHI volunteers and staff, during which there was no shortage of entertained and awe-struck exclamations, more than a hundred pieces of writing were selected for publication. Staff and volunteers went back into schools over the following weeks to work one-on-one or in small groups with students, helping them revise their pieces and connect these many stories into a collective narrative. Notes were taken, breakthroughs were made, and—on one memorable occasion—volunteers scaled a snow-wall to get to a class of eager eighth graders.

The work featured in this book is but a small sampling of the creativity, humor, and depth that met us in each and every classroom we visited. Plot points and character descriptions offered by innumerable students were instrumental in shaping additional prompts and stories throughout the project, and we were floored by the way in which students consistently inspired not only their classmates, but students in classrooms on the other side of the city. This book is a reflection of their many visions and the result is our most collaborative project to date. There is a sense of adventure in every student; and likewise, there is a sense of each of these students in the adventures you are about to read.

And what about our real heroes, the children who wrote this book? They continue to write and to share their creativity with the world around them. In this particular story—that of students of all ages and backgrounds working together to create an adventure—

there is no ending because it is an adventure that keeps on going. As new students pick up this book and apply their own imagination to the pages within, we know that the story continues. It continues further with every pencil they pick up, with every page that they fill. There are more stories to be told, and we look forward to the telling.

826CHI would like to issue countless thanks to the following Chicago Public Schools and teachers for participating in this project and allowing us to meet their brilliant students:

A. PHILIP RANDOLPH ELEMENTARY SCHOOL
7316 S. Hoyne Avenue
Sushma Lohitsa and Katina Moore

ELIZABETH P. PEABODY SCHOOL
1444 W. Augusta Boulevard
Peter Simpson

ELLEN MITCHELL ELEMENTARY SCHOOL
2233 W. Ohio Street
Lynn Riefenberg and Eric Woodland

ENRICO TONTI ELEMENTARY SCHOOL
5815 S. Homan Avenue
Maria Dussias-Cuevas and Mary Ann Kadow

ERIE ELEMENTARY CHARTER SCHOOL
1405 N. Washtenaw Street
Heidi DeVooght and Kevin Mitchell

JOHN B. DRAKE ELEMENTARY SCHOOL
2722 S. King Drive
Tijuana Bowen and Rick Coppola

HARVARD SCHOOL OF EXCELLENCE
7525 S. Harvard Avenue
Shari Hemesath

JONATHAN BURR ELEMENTARY SCHOOL
1621 W. Wabansia Avenue
Amy Bergeson and Carlos Patiño

HIRAM H. BELDING ELEMENTARY SCHOOL
4257 N. Tripp Avenue
Janine Nelson

JOSÉ DE DIEGO COMMUNITY ACADEMY
1313 N. Claremont Avenue
Pam Alexandroff, Elizabeth Rasgus, and Norma Zavala

JOSEPHINE LOCKE ELEMENTARY SCHOOL
2828 N. Oak Park Avenue
Marlene Alcantar and Marie Ruiz

PULASKI INTERNATIONAL SCHOOL OF CHICAGO
2230 W. McLean Avenue
Patricia Meza, Carol Navarro, and Anna Shane

PART 1

THROUGH THE EYES OF THREE

PROLOGUE

ALMA RODRIGUEZ, GRADE 5

This is a legend that has long been forgotten and a true story as well. You will learn many things along the way. The story is about the adventures of three friends and their creations. You will meet a boy who always tries to have fun no matter what. There is also a girl who uses her brains for everything she can. And finally, there is a lizard who loves science, invents many things, and takes everyone on a wonderful journey.

This story takes place in several locations. It has been told by many, but no one knows the true story. If you love chocolate, keep reading, because there's a big chocolaty adventure coming up. There is also a moment where one of the heroes travels to a certain country and plays a certain sport. (Whatever you do, don't touch the ball with your hands!)

Some people like to travel through what they read in books, some actually go around the world, and some just stay at home. The main characters go through all of this to find what they need, or what they *think* they want. Every location is peaceful—until the villain shows up, alone. He is not nice—he has an anger issue. He thinks throwing things at people is funny. He knows the key to getting to wherever the three friends want to go.

All over the world and in outer space, the three friends put their inventions together and try to beat the villain standing in their way. Read more if you dare to and figure out how everything starts. But beware if you keep reading, strange things will start to happen—if you start to float, it's because the story has headed to space in a spaceship.

SAM

NIA GIPSON, GRADE 8

Long ago, there lived a young boy named Sam, an intelligent girl named Ophelia, and a little lizard named Professor Stephen Scalious. They knew nothing of each other and they

lived in completely different worlds, but one thing they had in common was their desire for adventure. Little did they know this desire for adventure would bring them together and change their lives forever. It all started with young Sam, who yearned for something more.

On a very hot day in the burning pits of Tennessee, lived a small family of three. There was Ma, Pa, and little Sam, with their cat Venus. They ran a Brussels sprouts farm near Lake Swizzler (known for its unusual shape), but they had little business because no one liked Brussels sprouts. Ma and Pa were very kindhearted country folk, but they were strict about Sam's safety and nutrition. This is why they decided to grow Brussels sprouts.

When Ma was a little girl, she was never allowed to go outside and play, but when Pa was a little boy, he was always out with his friends and he would often have minor injuries. "It's a boy thing," Pa would always protest. But Ma did not like the idea of her little boy being hurt, so the only time Sam could go out was to help in the fields where Ma could watch him. She prevented Sam from having any fun.

"Sammy, now you know you can't go outside and run around. You might scratch your knee," Ma would always say. But every time Sam would try to tell her that he wouldn't play rough, she never cared to listen. The only other option for Sam was if he wore protective head and body gear so that he wouldn't get scarred. Sam did not like this idea very much. So every day Sam would play with his small, orange Siamese cat Venus, who Sam thought looked very similar to the planet.

Their friendship started one day when Sam was working in the fields. He found the cat scratching away at some Brussels sprouts with her razor sharp claws, trying to tear them apart. He knew right then that they would be the best of friends, because he hated Brussels sprouts, too.

To keep from dying of boredom, the two came up with a silly game: Venus bowling. Sam would line up jars of Brussels sprouts in a pin form, and Venus would roll into a ball and try to knock them all down. This was their favorite game, but of course sometimes Sam became frustrated because Venus would cheat every now and then. So Sam wanted to play with someone else. A human friend maybe, someone he knew wouldn't cheat.

As the long days went by with no Brussels sprouts business,

young Sam grew lonely, for no one wanted to be his friend. All of the kids in town thought he was weird because he would sleepwalk at night. Sam's sleepwalking had lead to several disasters. Many nights, for as long as the oldest one in town could remember, Sam walked all the way to Mr. Phickel's Pickle Shop, and once he ruined the store and then woke up the next morning with pickles in his bed. After that, no one wanted to be his friend.

Even though Sam didn't befriend many children in the town, nothing could take away from his love of adventure and his cleverness. After a long day of work, Sam would pretend he was a pirate sailing the seven seas like in the stories he was told. He would reenact all of the adventures he heard and the ones he wished to have and would turn them into a play. He would build ships and swords, make costumes, and create human-sized dolls that he used for his fellow merry men. Little did he know that his dreams would someday become reality.

Even with all this creativity, Sam was still lonely. His loneliness and curiosity drove him to sneaking out at night to look at the stars. Often, he would go out into the fields with Venus and look up at the sky to see the amazing view of stars. Sam loved the way they would sparkle and shine so bright, even though they were small and alone. They reminded him of what he wanted to be like.

Many times during his stargazing, Sam would see a shooting star and would make a wish with all of his heart. "Star light, star bright, the wishing star I see tonight; I wish I may, I wish I might, get the wish I wish tonight. Star, I wish that I could have a friend, a true friend. A friend who seeks adventure like I do, who wants to leave this miserable town. Someone I can talk to, who will be nice to me. Star, all I want is a great friend. Please, star, please."

Every night, Sam would call out to the stars and repeat this wish. One day, the stars finally answered him.

OPHELIA

DIANA LOPEZ, GRADE 7

When Ophelia turned three years old, she picked up a book from the bookstore's shelf and sat down on the nearest carpet and opened the book. Her mom, Arina, was near the cooking section. After a couple minutes, she realized that Ophelia wasn't near her. Arina looked like crazy for her! She even talked over the intercom: "Bring me my child! Her name is Ophelia and she is short and has one side of her hair curly and the other side straight. She has tan-colored skin and likes to walk in the rain. She has gray-colored eyes and she likes to wear lavender dresses."

Arina then went to the checkout section to ask if anybody had seen Ophelia. Suddenly Ophelia came out of nowhere and ran to her mom with a big book called *Everything You Need to Know About Cardboard* and said, "Mommy, are you getting ready to pay?"

Arina dropped everything she had in her hands. Relieved, she said, "Don't ever do that again! You almost gave me a heart attack!"

By the age of four-and-a-half, Ophelia had discovered she was good at inventions. She thought her skill was like everybody else's—normal. But it wasn't. Ophelia's parents knew that Ophelia was talented because everywhere in her room there were drawings of gadgets she wanted to create. Since her siblings broke everything in the house, she tried to repair them by creating new things.

One day, Ophelia was with her whole family in a computer repair shop, because her siblings were passing their computer around and one of them dropped it. Ophelia was waiting and watching TV and two different infomercials came on. One was about books for every age. The other was about computerized tablets. Ophelia got the idea of mixing both of those things together. She called her new eReader the "Bookie." While Ophelia waited at the shop, she continued to edit the Bookie. There, one of the workers saw it and suggested that they should call a leading technology firm to think about making her creation. From then on, the Bookie was a success.

By the time Ophelia was seven, she had five brothers and sisters, and most of them were younger than her. Her mom came up to her and said, "I need help."

Ophelia said, "With what?"

Her mom responded, "With taking care of the children, because I work the morning shift and Dad works the night shift. Also because everyone is allergic to something and I have to make different foods for each and every one of them." So Ophelia tried to help her mom take care of the kids by making a Foodinator that would give everyone food made especially for them, and would teach them how to be a bit more independent. It only helped for a couple days, because then they broke it. After that, Ophelia didn't do anything else for her siblings. She got so aggravated she decided she would start making plans to go somewhere else …

SCALIOUS

JAVON MACKEY, GRADE 8

This story is seen through the eyes of three. But let us tell you where it all began: In Wisconsin, in an aquarium under a plastic rock, there lived one who dreamt about seeing the outside world and gazing at the stars. He was one of the greatest minds in the world. He was the one, the only, Professor Stephen Scalious: a 5-foot lizard who loved poetry and science.

Before you get to the aquarium's plastic rock, you have to press the red pebble beside it to open it. Once inside, you will find a ladder that will take you down into what appears to be a deserted mine site. As you walk down the narrow hall, you will see lights that miners once used to light the way into what is now Professor Scalious's den. There you will find

pictures of his long-lost family, whom he does not remember much about, except when he last saw them on an island. All he can remember is that he had 250 family members. The picture with him being hatched by his mother near a body of water is a picture he's often left pondering about. Sometimes he thinks he was kidnapped from his family, because if you look really closely at that picture, you can see the eyes of some kind of cat hidden in the grass.

This picture is the main reason Professor Scalious likes science, because he uses scientific methods to figure out what kind of lizard he is and in which part of the world his kind can be found. So far he's found out he is some kind of rare Komodo dragon, which are only found in some parts of Asia.

Professor Scalious has never gone outside the aquarium before. So, lately, he has been doing some tests on the sun to develop a kind of chip he can put in his ear that helps his eyes adjust to the light much faster. He figures since his eyes are so used to the dark that if he goes outside he might go blind, or the sun could melt his brain and he won't remember who he is—and then he would be stuck living like a caveman.

Every time Professor Scalious thinks this about his future, he says to himself, "How obscure," or, "Just the thought is beneath me." He also developed a way to keep himself dry with what he calls "water sprout." It's a little seed he keeps in an airtight case because the seed turns into 10-feet of air all around him when he is underwater. So if he ever wants to leave the aquarium, he's well-prepared for the outside world.

PART 2

A GOOD PLACE TO
START AN ADVENTURE

OUT THE FRONT DOOR

AATIANA HUNTER, GRADE 3

By the time Ophelia was nine years old she knew she wanted to see more of the world than just her school. She knew if she behaved well, her parents would let her go to a place called The Boring Store on Saturdays to write stories. This was one of her favorite things to do—writing. She would always tell her parents that she wanted to be a writer. Her parents had a whole  bookshelf devoted to Ophelia's stories, but no matter how proud her parents were of Ophelia's talent, they still didn't approve of her going out by herself.

One night, Ophelia was lying in her bed thinking about what she would like to do tomorrow. She would go see something new! She got up that morning to eat breakfast but told her parents she wasn't hungry. Ophelia hurried to run out the front door when her parents said, "Where are you going, young lady?"

Ophelia said, "I'm just going to the barn to feed the horses."

"If you are going to feed the horses, why do you have that giant bag on your shoulder?" asked Ophelia's dad, Charles.

"The hay is in this bag, Father," said Ophelia.

"Let me see inside that bag. You're not going to feed the horses."

"Yes, I am, Father."

"If you're going to feed the horses, why do you have a camera and batteries? You're staying in the house."

"Father, I can't."

"Go to your room, young lady."

Ophelia stomped up the stairs with anger. She slammed the door behind her and took out one of her stories and started writing. When she finished writing, she thought to herself, "I will never be able to go *anywhere*..."

SAM DISCOVERS THE ISLAND

MIA BAEZ-VASQUEZ, GRADE 4

Sam had loved adventure ever since he went fishing with his dad when he was younger. His favorite types of adventures were the ones he got to go on alone because no one could boss him around.

One day, Sam had to go get water from the lake to water the Brussels sprouts. He thought this job was boring.

"I'm tired of eating Brussels sprouts," he snapped, talking to his cat Venus on his way to the lake. "We have to do it every night."

Venus didn't say anything. She just followed Sam.

Sam got to the lake and began to dip a bucket into the lake really fast and fell face-first into the water. Venus had pushed him from behind!

"Heeeey!" Sam yelled.

Just then, Sam looked up and saw something amazing. It was an island. At first he didn't believe his eyes because he had water in them and thought he was seeing things. But then he shook his head from side to side and saw that the island was still there. In the distance, he thought he saw a Ferris wheel!

"Whoaaa," Sam said. "What's that?!"

Sam got up and began to run over to Venus calling, "Hey, Venus! Let's go check it out!"

Just as he was about to catch up with Venus, Sam ran straight into his dad, who had come to check on him to see where the water was.

"Honey!" Sam's dad said to Sam's mom when he noticed the island. "Come see this!"

Sam's mom was planting Brussels sprouts in the field and walked down to the lake. When she saw the island, she asked, "Where did this come from?" She had a strange expression on her face that Sam thought was weird.

"Oh, can I go to it? Can I go over there?" ask Sam.

Sam's parents both said, "No. What if it's dangerous? We don't even know where that island came from."

After dinner, Sam got Venus and said to his parents, "I'm going to go plant some Brussels sprouts."

"I'm very proud of you," said his dad.

Sam just smiled, slipped out the door, and went down to the beach to find the family's canoe. They usually used it for fishing in the summer but tonight it was going to used for fun!

Sam canoed as fast as possible. The water was blue because of the moon and it was a little wavy. Sam didn't care but Venus was scared. She began to scratch the canoe, but then Sam reached into the water and caught a fish with his bare hand and gave it to Venus. After that, she was fine and busy enjoying her fish.

When they got to the island, it was like an amusement park! It had cotton candy, a Ferris wheel, and a secret part that was scary with rides you had to go on in the dark. Sam and Venus had this amusement park all to themselves.

After they discovered all the fun and cool things they could do without Sam's parents, they went to the amusement park every night, stuffing themselves with candy and going on their favorite rides, including the LOOOOOOPmeister which had six loops (one "O" for every loop), and then going back at sunrise before Sam's parents woke up.

One morning when Sam got back to his farm, he saw his parents waiting for him on the beach. They looked very angry and they were mad that he hadn't listened to them.

"You shouldn't go back there," Sam's mom told him. Then she told him the real story: Sam's great-great-great-great grandfather had built the amusement park years ago when he was a teenager and thought working on the farm was boring. Sam's parents thought his great-great-great-great grandfather was foolish for not working on the farm and they didn't want Sam to be like him.

"What if I want to be like him? What if I don't want to work on the farm? I want to have adventures!" Sam yelled, and ran to his room.

That night, and every night after that, Sam and Venus snuck out through their window, climbed down a tree, and headed to the island in the family's canoe. Sam brought along important things like toilet paper and a bucket for popcorn, and also Venus's stuffed fish toy.

Every night, as they were going to the canoe to return to the farm, Sam crammed his face with cotton candy and hid other candy in his pockets. Sam didn't even feel very bad about sneaking out because his parents always had him trapped on the farm. He always made sure to get back by dawn so they wouldn't know.

HE WAS DONE BEING AMATEUR

TAYLOR JACKSON, GRADE 6

"Professor" Stephen Scalious had a dream of becoming a professional scientist. He was indeed a very good amateur scientist, but amateur was just too—how you say—*little* for him. So one day he decided he was done being amateur. He went in his laboratory and said, "I'm going to create the best invention known to man...well, lizard, in my case."

Suddenly, he had the perfect idea. "I've got it!" he shouted. "I'll make a chemical to stop the growing of lizard predators. I'll have to start immediately!"

He began to look through his things.

"Okay, I have this, I have that, and of course *that*, and the main ingredient—wait, where did it go? That rare Peruvian pepper? Where is it? Oh, no! It took nearly two weeks to get these ingredients and twice as much time to get the Peruvian pepper. I'm doomed! It's going to take so much time. What am I going to do?" He thought a moment more. "Oh, I got it! The nature museum attached to the aquarium. There's that rare plant exhibit. I'll go there to get it myself."

He paused for a moment. "But I have no transportation! Why do things have to be so difficult?" Stephen paced back and forth thinking.

"Ah-ha! I got it! I'll go to Aunt Mary's. She will have to let me use her dune buggy."

Aunt Mary was Professor Scalious's adopted aunt. She had taken him in years ago when he had no real family of his own. Her house was down by the fake riverbank in the aquarium. It was made of rocks and held together by one little stick, with a piece of tree bark for a door. Stephen had not visited Aunt Mary in two years.

"Who knows if she will lend me her dune buggy?" he wondered. "Will she even speak to me? So many questions. It is just a couple of blocks away. How could I have been so inconsiderate? Well, off I go!"

It was hot and very sunny. Stephen walked the green path to Aunt Mary's house. It took 10 or 15 minutes, of course, with him having small feet and all. Finally, he was there!

Knock, knock, knock. The smell of apple pie was surrounding the whole house.

"Aunt Mary, it's me, Stephen."

"Oh, Stephen!" said Aunt Mary as she opened the door. "How are you?" she cried, and pinched his cheeks. "I haven't seen you in how long? Two years maybe? You look so skinny!"

"Yeah, Aunt Mary. Sorry about that."

"It's okay."

"I'm here to ask if I might be able to use your dune buggy."

"My dune buggy?"

"Yeah, the thing in the back."

"Hmm, I'll have to think about it," said Aunt Mary.

"But I don't have time for you to think about it. I need to get a very rare pepper. It will change the lives of many lizards."

"How about we have dinner, sweetheart, and I will think about it. My mind might change a little bit."

Professor Scalious had never been able to say no to Aunt Mary. Maybe it was just her sweet voice that was so persuasive. Or maybe he just couldn't say no to an old green woman. Hours passed with

Aunt Mary as she told him about the two years he had missed. She even told him about how a younger cousin grew his first chest hair and about how excited he was to see it. Professor Scalious guessed she was just trying to make up for those lost two years. Who knows, maybe she just needed company?

"Dinner's ready," Aunt Mary finally said.

It was baked worm with snail-slime gravy.

"Mmm, this is delicious, Aunt Mary."

"It's my new recipe," she said. "A touch of snail slime gives a good taste to baked worm."

Professor Scalious stuffed his mouth with baked worm and snail slime. "I'm done," he said with his mouth full. "Can I use the dune buggy now?"

"I suppose. A promise is a promise."

"Thank you, Aunt Mary. And I promise to come by more often."

"Well, you better, or you won't be able to try my new beehive soup with bumblebee dye!"

"Okay, bye!" Stephen said. He waved and headed off thinking about the Peruvian pepper.

As Professor Scalious drove along in the dune buggy he thought, "This sort of experiment will definitely make me more professional. People now will take me more seriously. Who *knows* what honor the people will give me? I might write a book on my fabulous adventure. They might even make me president. I've made chemicals where I could make lizards the color of their mood, but of course no one cares about color or true talent when they see it. I even made homemade fireworks that say names and it still didn't impress. People take me as a joke. But not for long!"

BOOGLEDORF, WHO WANTED A CRANKY WORLD

SARAH BREINIG, GRADE 6

Now you need to know who former-professor William Harold James Boogledorf III was. He was kind when he was born, but he was born into a grouchy family, so by the age of 4 he was evil and very, very grouchy. It wasn't his fault.

At age 2, he had read every book that was written in that time range, including comic books, history textbooks, adventure books, fantasy books, and any other book you can think of. He was now so old he had forgotten how old he *was*, but he somehow remembered all the useless facts he'd ever read. (He thought he was born on 12/17/1717, and this was why he liked the number "17.")

Even in disguise, Boogledorf could be recognized by his big eyes, big nose, large mouth, and small feet. His house was a jumbo garbage can (literally!) and it stunk like trash. It was so messy that all you could find in it was a bowl of stamps, his TV, and his rainbow couch, showing every color of the rainbow. Ever since Boogledorf had quit his job as a professor, he spent most of his time sitting on his couch and staring intently at his favorite TV show, *I Watch TV*, all day long. *I Watch TV* was a television show about a guy who watches TV, hence the name.

Boogledorf only wore one pair of clothes, because all his other clothes were lost amid all the garbage in his house. He didn't wear socks. He objected to socks, just to be grouchy. His bed was lost somewhere, too. His hair was very tangled—mainly because he prided himself on messy hair, but also because he couldn't find his comb, and he couldn't find his money to buy a new one. He hoped someday to find his wallet in the couch.

Boogledorf also hated cheese. *Hated* it. He hated it so much that he also hated the state most famous for making it: Wisconsin. Boogledorf liked cake, but who knew if that would change.

Once, Boogledorf and a fellow professor were trying to invent a way to make stamp glue taste better. Boogledorf tasted it first and was obsessed with it. He loved the stamp glue. He ate it all and made more. After his 111,111,111th bowl of stamp glue that held twenty tons each, he noticed how much he'd had. He got mad at the other professor for making him addicted to the lemon-flavored stamp glue, and he swore he'd "get" the other professor for this.

Most people didn't want to be around Boogledorf for more than .02 seconds, because they thought he was a disgusting slob. This made him feel more cranky, but he liked being cranky, so he liked that people didn't like him. He just got crankier and crankier and crankier. Some people thought Boogledorf would explode out of crankiness. He wanted a cranky *WORLD*.

THE AMATEUR SCIENTIST'S CHOICE AWARDS

BABY ANTUNEZ, GRADE 3

Professor Stephen Scalious was trying to decide what experiment would be right for the Amateur Scientist's Choice Awards. These awards were a worldwide contest for the best experiment. Every year, since Professor Scalious first won the award, five lucky scientists had been chosen for an experiment the judges find exciting.

Each winner got a red and yellow bag with $75,000, and the chance to be on TV. Every year, Professor Scalious went to the Scientist's Choice Awards, and some of his friends went to see him, too. It was easy for everyone to get there because the awards were held in the Wisconsin Blue Aquarium, where Professor Scalious lived.

At the awards, there was a big stage that was a square and had curtains. There were always a lot of people there, including the TV producers who put them on TV. All of the scientists were animals. Past winners had been bears, snakes, dogs, cats, a lizard (Professor Scalious), a gorilla, and a bird. They had built lasers to make the moon bigger, and had even proven you could make a Shrinkinator out of Jell-O.

This year, Professor Scalious was going to see if he could make a time machine that would help people visit the day they were born. If he could build that machine, he knew he would win.

HOW TO PRETEND YOU ARE A PROFESSOR:
Instructions from Professor Stephen Scalious

ANTHONY HUERTA, GRADE 4

If you are not actually a professor, but want to make it seem like you are, do the following steps in order:

1. First you have to be alive. If you are, the rest will be a breeze.

2. Buy a lab coat on sale. The lab coat should be white, because professors wear white lab coats (not polka-dot ones—unless chemicals were spilled).

3. Put on the lab coat. You should also have an undershirt on (in any color).

4. Buy ten beakers, at the science store or on eBay, and put

water in them with food coloring. most real scientists wouldn't know the difference between food coloring and chemicals. chemicals are different colors and a fake professor wouldn't want to mix them because it would cause an explosion in your face.

5. Buy a laboratory, or rent it from another fake professor. it should be full of beakers and other scientific stuff like extra lab coats hanging around.

6. Talk "scientific." Talk about things like earthquakes. you can talk about forces — just say some scientific words and they will think you're a professor.

7. The last step is to invite people (like other real professors) over and give them a tour of your lab. you have to do all of these steps exactly for people to believe you!

congratulations! you have graduated from fake professor school.

A FEW THINGS ABOUT ME

SHAKIYAH ASPHY, GRADE 6

Dear Diary,

I'm glad to finally have a diary. My mom gave it to me because I'm just about to turn 10 years old. A few things about me: I love reading books—it's so fun. Also, I have seven brothers and sisters.

My oldest sister Sarah is SUCH a teenager. She's fourteen. Every time I see her, she's on the phone or going out to parties and concerts—with boys, too. My mom gave her a phone and ever since she got it, she spends all her time talking on the phone with people at her school. She never notices that I'm always by the door to her room, hearing everything that she says about boys to her friends.

My oldest brother's name is Steve and he's 12 years old. He's very funny. I always laugh at his jokes. He has a joke book that he keeps in his room. I never noticed he was using it until I came in the house and he was reading a book called **Jokes**. I still thought he was funny, even though he was getting his ideas from a book.

Jeanne is 8 and likes to invent things. I'm a better inventor than Jeanne, so she got it from me. When I was making a microwave that made food when you pushed the button without you having to cook it, Jeanne saw it and wanted to be better with her own inventions. Jeanne already knew a little bit about how to invent things in her class, so one time I tried to help her learn a little more about inventions. She made a glow stick and threw it at me. I got  angry and told my parents, and they took away Jeanne's little science bottles and the colors in them that make things explode.

My second-oldest brothers' names are Byron and Bobby. They are 7 and twins. They love playing video games. I wonder if they will play them all their lives. Byron and Bobby are always trying to hog the TV. Me or my other brothers and sisters will want to watch our shows, but they always say, "I'll give it to you in a minute." When it's dinnertime, the twins are the first ones to get their plates, and when they are done, they're the first to go back to the TV.

My sister Mia is 5. She likes drawing and painting. One time, I made her paint me a picture by tickling her feet. I want her to make a drawing that says my name in pretty words. I think when she grows up, she's going to be a great artist and all of her paintings are going to be in fancy art museums.

My youngest brother is James. He is 3 years old and he loves singing and dancing. I wonder if he will ever get lessons because he is bad at singing, but the dancing is okay. He likes to make raps, but he is so bad that it makes us want to leave the house without him—we always cover our ears. One time, he told the whole family to sit down on the couch to hear him sing, but when I heard the first note, I covered up my ears. When he was done my parents said, "You're great honey, keep doing a good job."

I said, "Mom! Stop lying to him."

I told you about my brothers and sisters, but I'll see you later to talk more about me.

Until next time,
Ophelia

....

Sam found that the amusement park was only one small part of the island he had discovered. There were beaches, forests, and all sorts of trails—which meant all sorts of adventures, too. It wasn't long before he was finding ways to sneak off to the island at all times of day and night in search of new adventures.

....

SAM'S ISLAND ROUTINE

ADRIAN QUINTERO, GRADE 3

During most days, Sam spent time on his own special island. On this island, the palm trees were tall and straight as rulers, the sand was a bit grassy, and the water looked like blueberry ice cream. The thing Sam loved most about being on the island was going swimming without his parents calling him back to work on the farm. Even though the water looked like ice cream, it swam like seawater. In the lake, Sam felt good and free because he was alone. The only other creature on the island was his cat Venus. When he was alone on the island with Venus he had no worries.

Every day, Sam had his island routine. First, he would get himself breakfast. To do this, he had to climb WAY up to the top of the palm trees to get fresh coconuts. The palms would wave around in the wind, and when he looked down he could see the sand and his cat Venus (she looked very tiny from way up there). He was pretty scared, but it was worth it. Fresh coconuts are sweet and refreshing.

After he took care of his breakfast it was time to get breakfast for Venus. Even though Venus was a cat, she liked the water sometimes, but Sam still did the fishing for her. He would put on goggles, flippers, and a snorkel and hunt for a tuna fish for Venus. Since he could see underwater with the goggles, he could always find one in no time.

After they both had their breakfasts, Sam would spend time looking for shells. His favorites were dried out starfish, because they reminded him of the stars. Then he liked to play catch with himself, throwing a big, red, white, and blue ball high in the air. Sometimes Venus would try to play, too, but she was a little too small.

The two of them spent a lot of time on a big sand project. They built four houses for friendly ladybug families that lived in the sand. Every day, the waves would go up and down and destroy the houses. Sam and Venus helped the ladybugs by rebuilding the houses. He built big boats, too—big enough to carry Sam and Venus across the water. And he built small villages from starfish shells, where he and Venus would sit.

At the end of each day, Sam would take a long swim in the lake. When he got out, he was cold and would head home to his parents where he liked to eat apples and strawberries for dinner.

A BIT MORE ABOUT BOOGLEDORF

LIO NUNEZ, GRADE 7

William Harold James Boogledorf III had telekinesis, which he used to grab stuff while he watched TV and movies (examples: drinks, snacks, pillows, blankets). And most of all, he was also a human almanac. His older brother, Walter Harold James "Smartypants" III, was a human encyclopedia. Boogledorf became evil because at first he didn't know many facts, and wanted to show his brother that he could be just as good as he was.

Boogledorf was his own idol because he knew a lot of facts.

He loved to follow people around and tell them useless facts constantly. It made him a pretty good super-villain because he never gave up. He selected people at random, and then he followed a single person for a whole week and told them ten facts a day. This was really annoying, because Boogledorf was repetitive and the facts he shared would never help anyone.

Useless facts Boogledorf had shared with strangers included:

- how many floors are in the tallest building in Dubai
- the number of grains in an exotic wood
- how much things would cost from a grocery store from the 1940s
- the fifth person who died in World War I and who shot him and the exact setting
- which toothpastes are not approved by the F.D.A.
- the actual shape of a star
- movie facts (on weekends)
- TV facts (on weekdays)

Everyday, Boogledorf hooked his brain up to a hard drive and copied his memory to it just in case he lost his own memory. He'd been banned from any academic event or competition because he always won, and no one else could. Also, he could never tell a lie or tell when someone else was telling a lie because his brain was so full of facts that he couldn't comprehend what a lie is.

....

Another thing you should know about Professor Scalious—he was a bit of a Renaissance lizard. Not only did he love science, he also loved poetry. Sometimes he found a way to combine the two.

THE EXPERIMENT:
A Poem by Professor Stephen Scalious

IVAN PEREZ, GRADE 5

I am professor scalious.
Around me are leaves, my science tools,
and my glasses.
The yummy smell of rotting fish meat
makes me hungry and my stomach growls.
(I like to eat dried flies and gooey water.)
I hear people and animals.
I touch my tools, and my rock bed is hard and bumpy.
I dig through to my hidden laboratory, lifting
the branches and wormy dirt away
to reveal the door that squeaks like a rat.
The chemicals bubble up inside the beakers and now
I am ready for the experiment to begin.

TIRED OF HER BROTHERS' AND SISTERS' TRICKS

CATHLEEN RAMIREZ, GRADE 3

Ophelia's brothers and sisters picked on her because she was smart and she was one of the oldest. She got all the new toys and clothes because of this, but the younger ones didn't get those things because they were little. Ophelia felt really sad and mad because her brothers were picking on her. When they did this, she was usually so mad that she stomped her foot and went running to her room.

It was a Friday, and Ophelia's birthday was Saturday. Ophelia went to her mother and asked her if she was going to have a party.

"Mom, am I going to get a birthday party? It's been a long time since I've had one," she cried.

Her mother said, "Yes! Go to bed, Ophelia."

Ophelia felt really excited. She went to bed. But when she got there, her brothers and sisters had stolen all her blankets. She felt really angry, as angry as when her brothers played all their other tricks on her.

The next day was Ophelia's birthday party. All of her cousins and aunts went to her birthday party. There were a lot of pink, red, blue, and white balloons, birthday hats, a lot of colored tablecloths, and pizza.

Ophelia felt really surprised.

"Wow!" she said.

When it was time to cut the cake, they opened the box where the cake was supposed to be, but there was nothing inside. Ophelia felt really angry again and started to think that her brothers were playing another trick on her. But because she was so smart,

Ophelia asked her mother to give her some money and then ran to the bakery down the block.

When she got to the bakery she asked, "Can you make a medium strawberry birthday cake really fast?"

The baker asked, "Do you want me to write your name on top of the cake?"

"Yes, please," Ophelia said.

Ophelia had to wait 30 minutes. Then she grabbed the cake and went running home—but slowly, because of the cake.

She got there and said, "The cake is all ready. Here! We can cut it now."

Her brothers and sisters were mad because their plan didn't work, and the next day Ophelia's mother punished them. When their punishment ended, they played another trick on Ophelia. They wrote all over Ophelia's homework and all over her library book, called *Where the Elephant Lived in the Home*. She liked the

book so much—it was her favorite book since she was little. She loved the elephants and imagined they lived in her house.

Her brothers and sisters wrote her name on all the pages in black marker. Ophelia felt really sad. When she went to return the book to the library, she had to pay the library fine with all the money she had saved to buy her very own copy of the book.

Ophelia was tired of her brothers' and sisters' tricks. She talked to them and said that it was bad behavior to play tricks on her.

She said, "Why are you guys playing tricks on me? I don't really do anything to you guys. I talk to you, but I don't bother you."

Ophelia's brothers and sisters all said that they would never play another trick on Ophelia. They all played together instead and they played a lot of games, and for a while they never fought. Ophelia felt really happy, but she was still worried they would play tricks on her again. She wanted to try to relax in another place.

CATCHING STARS

EMILY ALVARADO, GRADE 2

Sam sometimes imagined that if he could catch a bright star, he would love to play with it. So one night he said, "Hey, Venus, do you want to go on a hunt?" Venus purred happily and loudly.

They walked for a while looking up at the stars and they ran fast to grab one. Sam had built the tallest building on the island and he and Venus slept in it some nights. When they got to Sam's building, Sam grabbed his butterfly net from his bedroom and they climbed the stairs to the roof. Sam swung the net to try to catch the brightest star and he almost caught it but it was too high in the sky. Venus jumped up on the edge of the roof and swatted with her paw to try to catch it, too. Sam  laughed at the cat trying to catch the star and Venus looked at Sam like he was crazy and jumped down.

Near the corner of the roof, Sam had put a brand new, gray trampoline, so Sam grabbed Venus in his hands and climbed on it. He started jumping until he was high and closer to the star. Sam jumped and jumped but he couldn't catch the star. This made him angry. Then he remembered his butterfly net, so he put Venus down on the ground and took the net in his hands.

He jumped and jumped and reached and reached with his net until he grabbed the star. Sam exclaimed, "Yes! I got the star!"

Sam was so happy. He held that star gently in his hands. He walked back down to his room. He took a jar from the table and put the star in it. Then he put the lid back on.

"Look, Venus, I got the star and now it has a home."

BOOGLEDORF AND OPHELIA MEET

CHEROKEE SPERRY, GRADE 6

As we know, William Harold James Boogledorf III had once been a normal man. Well, pretty normal. But one day, he had a craving for cake. He went to a bakery called The Bakery. Ophelia and her mother were working at The Bakery. Ophelia loved her part-time job there, after elementary school. She thought it was awesome, because she got to use her science skills.

Ophelia was hired to experiment on cakes. She was hired to make a prank cake for April Fool's Day. They were working on a marrow-flavored cake, a lamb's-blood-flavored cake, a beef-stew-flavored cake, and a sausage-flavored cake. But her current project was an earwax-flavored cake.

Boogledorf bought a yellow cake and walked out of the store. Little did he know, the yellow cake was part of the experiment! When he took a bite of the cake, he immediately spat it out again.

In a rage quite unlike himself, he ran back to the bakery and demanded, "Who made the cake?!"

Ophelia's mother told him that her daughter, Ophelia, invented the cake.

"Let me at her!" Boogledorf screamed, as spit cascaded out of his mouth.

"No," stated Ophelia's mother, sternly.

"Then I want a refund!"

"Sorry sir, our store policy is no refunds on experimental baked goods." And with that, Boogledorf launched the cake at her face and swore he would get revenge on Ophelia.

As he was leaving, Boogledorf stated, "Sand was often in ancient Egyptian bread," and then walked out casually, as if nothing had happened.

Since that time, Boogledorf had been in training. He had even made himself a villain costume, a pink-spandex-jumpsuit-type deal. Every morning, he did a five-mile run and baked many sponge cakes to practice throwing, so that he could someday get revenge on Ophelia by throwing a cake at her and winning back his honor.

SAM'S FIRST DAY OF SCHOOL

MINA NUNEZ, GRADE 6

It was the first day of school for Sam. It was Sam's *first* day because his mom was very protective of him so she usually taught him at home. But Sam wanted to meet other people and make friends so he begged his mom to let him go to school. She finally just gave up and let him go—as long as he promised not to get hurt.

As he got closer to the schoolyard, Sam saw a big huge red brick building with lots of doors that looked to him how he had always pictured school. A few kids turned to stare at him.

Even though he'd asked to go, Sam hated to be the new kid at school because he didn't make friends easily. It was hard for Sam to make friends, since he was "different." That's what people would say. Sam felt like he was a regular 11-year-old boy with short brown hair and green eyes. His parents told him he was unique, not strange or weird. He had good talents like creativity, writing, and drawing, but people didn't see that. Other kids didn't understand his artwork—like it was a mystery or something. They were more interested in comic books.

Sam was on his way to his classroom. He could smell lunch coming from the cafeteria and hear people talking in the hallways. They were all talking about some new kid coming to school, but he didn't realize it was *him*. Sam noticed a long row of blue lockers that had locks on the knobs. He wondered what the lockers were for—he didn't really get the point of them. He kept on wandering through the school until a supervisor gave him a paper with his room number on it.

"Thank you," Sam said, and walked to the classroom.

He had just walked in when his teacher, Mr. Kyle, said, "Class, we have a new student."

Sam took a seat. Mr. Kyle told Sam to introduce himself. Sam was excited, but he didn't like being put on the spot, so he just froze for a second. Slowly he walked to the front of the classroom and mumbled, "My name is Sam." Then he quickly sat back down at his desk. The whole class just stared blankly at Sam. Then they continued their work. Sam was relieved, and thought, "Okay, I don't have to be put on the spot anymore."

Sam had an assignment to create a short story and he had to share it with the class. This was easy for Sam since he had such a great imagination. When he finished writing, Mr. Kyle asked Sam to share his story first. He got up, feeling a little nervous, and read his story, which he called *An Adventure to Remember*. It was based off a dream he had.

When he was done reading, the class stared at Sam again. A girl named Ophelia said, "Nice job." The rest of the class made fun of him, even though his story was very good. They were just jealous because of how creative he was. But Ophelia sat next to him and introduced herself.

"I think your story was really good, Sam, it was better than mine. Don't worry about the class, they're just jealous," Ophelia said.

Sam felt happy. The girl seemed like a nice person, and he finally had something nice said to him instead of just glares from the class.

"Thanks, Ophelia," Sam said.

The two of them began talking. Sam asked her about her life and how she lived, and she asked him more about how he lived. As they talked, the realized they were not so different. Ophelia also had trouble making friends because people sometimes made fun of the way she talked. They would make fun of her sometimes and call her a nerd.

"But for me, being called a nerd is kind of a good thing, because I like being smart," she said. "But I wish that people would sometimes say 'Good Job' instead of saying stuff like 'Way to go, nerd.'"

"Ophelia," said Sam, "you're the smartest person I know. And the nicest person I've met."

Ophelia smiled at Sam. "Wow, a compliment," she thought. "Sam and I will probably be good friends."

That afternoon, the class had a bunch of math problems to work on. Sam didn't really understand the math too well, but Ophelia explained it to him—while other people might have just thought he was stupid.

Because nobody was sitting by Sam, Ophelia sat next to him for the rest of the day. Sam talked about more of his dreams with Ophelia. They were excited to find out that they both wanted to go on adventures instead of living a boring life.

By the end of the day, Sam and Ophelia started to become best friends. They made plans the next day to meet at a hideout by the school and start planning an adventure.

BOOGLEDORF AND SCALIOUS MEET

SOPHIA WILLIAMS, GRADE 6

The Wisconsin Blue Aquarium was not a place many people bothered to go to. In fact, only about a thousand people came to the bland and boring aquarium every year. It was a calm place, where visitors' voices were just like the creatures in the tanks: mellow. One of the creatures was a little green lizard named Stephen Scalious, who—despite his tiny size—was actually pretty famous, since he was the official mascot of the state of Wisconsin. In fact, his face appeared all over the state, on billboards, flyers, and even in skywriting. The governor picked Scalious as the state's mascot because he was impressed by the lizard's science skills and the many Amateur Scientist's Choice awards he had earned. On top of that, that governor favored his charisma. Scalious was almost a hippie—all love and no war.

Then there was William Harold James Boogledorf III, who wasn't exactly the kindest person on the planet. From the age of seven, he was destined to become a super-villain. He would often run around his room wearing a Joker costume. Years later, Boogledorf became a grim, wrinkly old monster, but he still ran around his cobweb-filled apartment in that now-skintight Joker costume.

For some odd reason, Boogledorf never seemed to like the state of Wisconsin, maybe because they like cheese more than cake there. On the day of May 27th, Boogledorf was going to visit Wisconsin's smallest aquarium, Wisconsin Blue, with a sinister plan in mind. His mission was to capture Wisconsin's state mascot, Scalious, and leave Wisconsin's people without an icon to represent their state.

Coincidentally, May 27th was also the birthday of Scalious's best friend, a chameleon identified as Juju. The poetry-and-science-loving lizard decided he would escape from under his plastic rock and run to the rain forest section of the aquarium to wish Juju a very happy birthday.

At around 2:30 p.m. the security guards dozed off, during yet another day absent of any visitors. Scalious began to scale the Plexiglas windows of his tank that barricaded him from reaching the sweet, cheesy air. Scalious was shaking with fear and excitement as he reached the top of the tank. Slowly his long, sticky fingers grasped the edge and he pulled himself to freedom.

His vast, bulging eyes peeked around to see if anyone was coming. The answer was no. His minute legs bent down to jump from the edge of the tank and on to the linoleum floor. The skitter-skatter tapping of his tiny feet barely echoed through the halls, like the sound of rain falling softly against a window.

Scalious was filled with ecstasy. However, with no sudden warning, a man with crazy gray hair turned the corner, mumbling about cake. It was Boogledorf. He quickly spotted a green dot running down the hall and chased after it.

The sound of heavy breathing crunched into Scalious's ears. A man was running after him. Scalious tried to speed up, but he was exhausted. A large, pale, veiny hand reached down and grabbed Scalious in the middle of his tiny body.

"I got you now!" Boogledorf cried. By chance, Boogledorf had a red velvet cake in his pocket, and he whipped it at Scalious.

"What was that for?" Scalious asked, his face covered in cream cheese frosting.

"I HATE WISCONSIN!!" Boogledorf growled back.

"Why are you taking it out on me?" asked the lizard, panting for air in the man's grip, which was tightening like a boa constrictor.

"I have no one else to take it out on."

"Well, then," said Scalious. "I'll be going now."

Scalious finally wriggled his bright green body out of Boogledorf's clenched hand, and scampered into the darkness of the halls, returning to his tank.

Boogledorf was filled with anger and envy. His thoughts were racing about ways to recapture Scalious.

"Why, now the lizard has given me time to think about my plan," Boogledorf said to himself.

Scalious's heart was racing with fear, as was his mind. He began to think in his tank.

"Why, oh *why*, would that man want to capture me?! I've never done anything to *anybody*!" Scalious was frantically writing a poem on his foot, recalling his experience with the crazy man and his crazy, tangled grey hair. Scalious persisted on his quest to wish his chameleon friend a happy birthday, and no crazy man was going to stop him.

As Scalious climbed up his tank walls, he remembered just how important it was to wish Juju a happy birthday. Ever since they were youngsters, they had celebrated each other's birthdays by making tomato-peach cupcakes. This tradition had had been going on for years, ever since Juju's 14th birthday, when Scalious gave him his favorite kind of chameleon bronze juice. It was the exact thing Juju had wanted for 14 years, and then he had gotten it from Scalious. After that, they were best friends.

Reality snatched Scalious back to the present, as an insane man was waiting beyond the corner. Scalious was careful this time to avoid the man he had initially encountered. He leaped over the rim and jogged to the corner Boogledorf was hiding behind. He didn't make it in time. Boogledorf's left arm whipped around and tossed a strawberry-stuffed cannoli right into Scalious's oddly-shaped head. The shell cracked and the filling coated his face.

Scalious's sight was disabled and he was not able to retaliate. He was very vulnerable. Nothing and no one could save him now. Scalious did not know Boogledorf's weakness, so he wasn't sure how to disable him. Boogledorf finally had the Wisconsin Blue mascot right in front of him. A smirk was plastered onto his face, and the lizard could not even see where he was. The strawberry filling was so thick, Scalious was practically blind.

But then he quickly saw a flash of yellow. As it passed, it smeared the frosting off his face. Scalious recognized the color and automatically knew it was his beloved friend Juju, one of the hairiest chameleons known to chameleon-kind. In his left hand, Juju had a black large-tooth comb. Juju swung around and quickly combed Boogledorf's hair. Combs were Boogledorf's greatest weakness. That's why his hair was such a monstrosity.

"Noooo! My masterpiece of messy hair. Gone!" the old, grim monster yelled. The untamed hair now lay flat and regular. It hung low by his shoulders.

Juju had come to Scalious instead of Scalious coming to Juju. Scalious could now wish Juju a happy birthday—but not before a shriek echoed through the hallways.

"I will make my hair a mess once again and finish what I started!" Boogledorf yelled as he hobbled out through the front doors, disappearing from Wisconsin.

Now Scalious could really wish Juju a happy birthday.

"Happy Birthday, to the best bronze-juice-drinking, hairiest chameleon ever!"

Professor Scalious's run-in with Boogledorf had really shaken him up. For a while he couldn't sleep at night, and when he finally did, he had strange dreams of far-off places...

WHAT WOULD BE MY DESTINY:
An Entry in Professor Stephen Scalious's Dream Journal

NIFEMI OLUGBEMIGA, GRADE 7

The intensity was building up. I could feel the heat bursting out of my body as I ran as fast as I could. I couldn't hear the screaming fans or the coach yelling from the sidelines. All I could hear was the beating drum in my chest and the sound of my breathing as the rain poured down.

The score was one to nothing. All I needed was one shot and we would go into overtime. players would come at me, but no one could get the ball away. I was so in the zone. My head was totally focused on the game.

Every second I was closer to what would be my destiny. As I approached the goal, I took a quick glance at the crowd. My eyes wandered and then I froze. A creature like my own caught my attention. She was slender with beautiful white pearls around her neck. She

was walking toward me. As her eyes met mine time seemed to freeze, and it made my head sing harmonies.

"Mamacita, what is someone like you—"

The thunder woke me up. It was just a dream. I looked around to remember where I was. I lived in Wisconsin under a plastic rock in an aquarium.

"Why am I here?" I asked myself. It seemed the reasons I was here had no meaning whatsoever. I had to leave to find myself.

Ophelia and Sam had been thrilled to find each other at school. They knew right away they were meant to be best friends, and they planned to have all sorts of adventures together. What they didn't plan on was that the very next day after they met, Ophelia would skip six grades and go to high school.

OPHELIA'S FIRST DAY OF HIGH SCHOOL

LORENZO HARRIS, GRADE 6

It was Ophelia's first day–she couldn't stop thinking about how nervous and excited she was to be in high school. Even when she was getting ready that morning her mother told her, "You don't have to go, you know. You can stay in elementary school or even middle school." But Ophelia still wanted to go because she liked challenges.

A small part of her didn't really want to go because she already missed her new friend Sam. She had been so excited to meet him and now she had no idea when she would see him again. She was also nervous she would feel out of place in high school. Ophelia wondered if the work would be too hard for her. Every time she thought about high school it was like being a cheerleader completing the pyramid. It could all come crashing down.

The first thing Ophelia noticed when she walked into school was how high the ceilings were. She was amazed to see a lot of things happening at once. Everyone was so *tall*. The jocks of the school walked with a lean to the side and the cheerleaders went down the hallway like runway models. As Ophelia walked down the hallway, the most embarrassing thing happened. Out of nowhere, when she wasn't paying attention, she slipped and fell. Her books flew everywhere. Everyone saw and laughed. Ophelia got up and ran to the nearest door.

The small, dark room turned out to be a janitor's closet. While she was in the closet she kept thinking: "I should have listened to my mom! I should have listened to my mom! If I weren't here I would never have slipped. No one would be laughing and I would still be in boring elementary school."

Classes were just about to start when the janitor opened the door. The light shined on Ophelia's foot, which was stuck in a bucket. She tried to get her foot out while heading to class. The janitor tried to help her, but she kept walking down the hallway with the bucket clunking along. She couldn't help hearing her mother sassing her: "You wanted the challenge." This was Ophelia's worst day ever.

Walking into class late with the bucket still on her foot, she tried to sneak in. Her teacher, Mr. Scott, caught her. He knew how smart she was and treated her special.

"Oh, Ophelia, don't worry. You don't have detention," he assured her.

Pretty soon half the day was gone, and it was time for lunch. The lunchroom is a place for food fights. Maybe not *all* lunch ladies serve bad food, but in this lunchroom the food had flies on it. Ophelia usually liked eating broccoli, but what she had didn't even look like broccoli. She tried to taste it, to see if it was just a little bit good. Like a gerbil, she took a nibble. She actually liked it! Everyone turned around and looked.

"You like the lunch lady's food?!" they asked.

In the background Ophelia could hear the lunch lady's voice. "At least someone likes my food." She went over to the lunch lady and said, "You have got to give me the recipe to this."

"Hi. My name is Helga. It's nice to meet you, honey."

"My name is Ophelia. At first I wanted to leave school, but you just made my day great."

Helga invited Ophelia back into the kitchen. "Come on in."

Ophelia pointed over at a casserole that had been sitting there for a week. It had turned greenish-brownish and was covered in hair. She asked, "Can I try that?"

"Honey, you don't want that. I'm saving that for the principal. I put a little something in there for him." Helga gave a little taste of it to Ophelia anyway. It smelled horrible, but when she tasted it, she liked it.

"Oh, honey, I've got more of that in the fridge."

It's kind of odd to have a lunch lady as a friend. Ophelia loved her food too much. She felt connected to it.

"This food is way better than even what Iron Chefs can make," Ophelia said. "This is great."

Out of nowhere, the principal walked in. He had a crush on Helga and always tried to sweet-talk her. As he walked over, Helga said to Ophelia, "Don't tell him I was here." Helga ran into the bathroom to hide.

The principal lowered his glasses to the end of his nose because he thought it made him look handsome. Looking over his shoulder with his back to Ophelia he asked, "What are you doing later?" As he pushed his glasses back up, he was caught off guard. He tried to play it off and said, "Oh, oh, Oh-phelia! How is your homework going?"

"Okay," said Ophelia. "I've got to go to my next class." She walked away with the bucket still clunking on her foot. She started thinking to herself that this was an okay day and she was already looking forward to tomorrow. The only problem would be to figure out how to fit the bucket into her mom's car.

When Sam got to school the day after he met Ophelia, he was shocked to learn that she had gone to high school. Even though they had just met, he missed his new friend and wondered if they would ever meet again. School days felt long to him without her there, and he began spending more and more time on his island. Venus tried her best to cheer him up, but for a while it seemed nothing would work.

SAM DISCOVERS HIS TALENT

DERRELL KILLINGSWORTH, GRADE 6

One day on the island, Sam and Venus were sitting on the sand eating apple pie. There was a table behind them, but they preferred sitting on the beach. They really liked the feel of the sand. They were enjoying small pieces of pie, but they were getting full. Except for coconuts, they only ate dessert on the island because it was the only food around. At first this was fun, but they were starting to wish they had something else to eat.

"I am so bored today," Sam said to his cat Venus.

Venus looked at Sam and meowed, meaning, "Do you want to have seconds?"

"Nope, I'm full. But I do want to know something," Sam said. "What is your talent, Venus?"

Suddenly, Venus stood on the table behind them and started singing, "La la la la la la la laaa!"

"Oh, *singing*. That's your talent?" Sam asked.

Venus looked at Sam and began meowing again. Sam knew this meant Venus wanted to know what his talent was.

"I don't know," Sam said.

Venus meowed and seemed to want Sam to try to sing.

"Okay, but you'll be sorry!"

Sam stood up, cleared his throat, and sang terribly. It sounded like someone scratching a chalkboard.

"Stop, stop, *stop*!" meowed Venus. Venus couldn't help feeling sorry for Sam.

Sam looked ashamed. His face had a frown and his eyes drooped.

"I guess I don't have a talent," he said. Sam was disappointed in himself.

Venus jumped up on a rope that was hanging between two trees above them. It was an old rope that had turned a brownish color but it was still holding strong. Ever since they came to the island, Venus had jumped up on the rope to take naps. It was her favorite nap place because it gave her a chance to show her agility.

As soon as Venus landed on the rope, she started purring and falling asleep. But Sam was still thinking about their conversation and still wanted to talk to Venus.

"Venus! Hey, Venus, come down!"

Sam was trying to get her attention, but she was already asleep.

Sam decided to do something he'd never done before. He began to climb the tree that held one end of the rope.

The tree was a palm tree about 20 feet tall. As he climbed, he noticed pieces of bark sticking out, and he felt the trunk of the tree curving away from the rope. He began to feel nervous, and as he looked down in fear, he noticed how high he was off the ground.

Sam just kept telling himself he could do it, and before long, he was halfway to Venus.

When Sam got to the rope, he stepped onto it carefully. The rope stayed straight, so he decided he would go for it. At first, he had to stick his arms out to keep his balance and then he got nervous again, but after he started to walk across, he realized it wasn't as hard as it looked. Sam was proud of himself—he was accomplishing something big. He was going not too fast and not too slow and before long, he got to Venus. When

he reached her, he grabbed her and tossed her into a soft patch of sand as a joke.

From the ground, Venus saw Sam balanced on the rope. She was surprised to see that Sam was so good at it. So she climbed back up the tree and she meowed to Sam, "I think that's your talent."

When Sam made it back down to the ground, he thought about what Venus said and agreed it was his talent. For now, tightrope walking was fun, but Sam knew that one day he could use his talent for something greater.

The next day when they were eating breakfast, Sam and Venus were talking about what had happened the day before. Sam wanted to learn how to be a professional tightrope walker. So he rowed his boat off of the island and found a circus. He saw the tightrope walkers flipping on the ropes and wanted to learn how to do it himself. He introduced himself to one of the tightrope walkers and they soon became friends. They taught each other what they knew. Sam eventually learned how to tightrope walk like the professionals. He went back to the island and practiced on the rope that was there. He got better and better each day and soon he went back to the circus and joined them sometimes. He became one of the main attractions and he was much-loved for his tricks and flips.

Professor Scalious couldn't shake the feeling that something was missing in his life. He wanted...more. But what? Maybe a change of scenery would do the trick. But leaving the aquarium seemed like an enormous task, so he thought he'd have to bring the scenery to him!

HOW TO REDECORATE YOUR HOUSE:
Advice from Professor Stephen Scalious

ANGELINE MEDINA AND VICTORIA CORTEZ, GRADE 4

One day as I was lying near the sun in the petting zoo section of my aquarium, I looked around my brown plastic rock house and whispered to myself, "Ugh, my house is so ordinary. I want to liven it up." I decided I would gather supplies from the aquarium's arts and crafts center.

First, I grabbed the mint green, scarlet red, and aquamarine blue paints—all of my favorite colors. Then, I got a needle, yarn, cotton balls, and silky fabric. I also took paintbrushes, pencils, and paper off the shelf and carried them home to my tank. On the way, I saw Coco the hamster, who offered to help me.

When we got back to the rock, I turned on the music I use for yoga, which I like to do to relax. Then we had to move stuff around and make a plan (a.k.a. a blueprint). Coco said that when you redecorate stuff, you can move as you go, so we just moved it to one corner. I thought I might buy a bookshelf, or get some wood and make one.

Coco, a great artist, sketched pictures of the Eiffel Tower, the Sears Tower, and pyramids on the wall. I dipped the brushes in the paint and made polka-dotted spirals on the ceiling. Then I threaded the yarn in the needle and stuffed the shiny fabric to make fluffy lanterns. It was night by this time, so Coco and I went to the insect display and caught lightning bugs in a net, put them in a jar, and placed them in the fluffy lantern houses so I might have some light to complement the whole room.

This is how I turned my brown plastic rock into a home. When we were done, I had a green and wonderful rock.

....

Professor Scalious had to admit—his rock was rockin'. But it wasn't quite what he was after. Little did he know he'd find the answer that very day...

....

SCALIOUS MAKES A PLAN

EMILY BERMUDEZ, GRADE 6

Professor Scalious was cleaning his science equipment after his latest experiment. He was doing this with a special towel he had created that sprayed any cleanser he needed. A lot of his experiments and inventions were like this—things that were useful all the time. As he cleaned up, he thought to himself, "I do this every day. It's getting a little dull."

"Hmm," he thought, "maybe I could finally try something new. Maybe...I could be an artist!"

He tried doing a paint-by-numbers kit, but instead of being a dog like it was supposed to, it actually turned out to be a bad-looking horse.

"Oh, gosh, I'm a horrible artist!" he moaned. "I'm certainly no Coco."

He thought he might try cooking instead. After all, he was getting a little tired of having bugs every day, and maybe he could learn to cook something new, like pasta.

He got the ingredients he needed, but when he was done, something had gone wrong. The mostaccioli he was trying to cook looked like a big watery blob of feathers with meatballs on top.

"Maybe I could try it," he thought. "But I'm not going to like this."

He poked the blob with a fork and it began to move. He gulped and tried it anyway.

"AHHHHHHH! This. Is. Horrible!" he yelled. He scrubbed out his mouth with his special towel, which shot out mouthwash. When he finished he said, "I guess cooking is not for me."

Professor Scalious decided he would have to think of another plan.

He crawled into the darkest corner of his plastic rock and took out his flashlight and a book titled *Learn About the World Children's Atlas*. He'd got it from one of his pen pals who lived in Minnesota. They wrote to each other every day, and his friend had mailed the atlas as a gift. Professor Scalious had had the book sitting right on top of his rock for over a year, but he'd never really taken it out and looked at it. It was covered in dust from sitting out so long.

Professor Scalious was fascinated by the maps, because he had never seen anything like them before. He loved learning the shapes of the states, which looked to him like funny circles and squares and rectangles and even some shapes he didn't know. The book also showed him the mountain ranges and the different continents around the world. It showed where the deserts and oceans and lakes and rivers were, and how they were all different. He could even see maps with different symbols that told him interesting things, like where wheat and corn were grown.

When Scalious flipped to the cities section of the book, his eyes popped.

"This is *it*!" he cried. "Maybe instead of cooking or being an artist, I could go and *SEE* all of this!"

He decided to go around the world. That way, he could see new cites and learn new languages and meet new people—maybe even meet some friends along the way who might be interested in travelling around the world, too.

Since he was a scientist, Professor Scalious decided he would make a map that went all around the world, but he would travel underground.

"I bet nobody has tried this before," he said. "People usually go around the world in hot air balloons, trains, or cars, but I'll be the first one to dig a tunnel around the world. I can show the continents and states from underground and make a *tunnel* map! Maybe I could use this book to help me."

Professor Scalious was getting really excited about going on his trip, and he began to work on some new inventions and experiments that would help him along the way. As he finished creating gloves that would protect his hands from the digging, his heart was racing.

"Oh, my gosh!" he cried, "I can't believe this is happening!" He smiled and said, "The best day of my life will start in three days."

PREPARING TO 'ROUGH IT'

LARONE BRIM, JR., GRADE 7

Professor Scalious knew that he didn't know the first thing about surviving anywhere other than his rock at the aquarium. So he packed food for three days and prepared to rough it.

The first thing he did was break out of his compartment so he could find out more about his species, because he'd been out of touch. He salvaged food and water for the trip: food pellets and some of his other favorite foods, like leaves and small fish like anchovies. He brought recipes with him so he could make food on the go, and decided he would look for a new pellet recipe because the old one was yucky—it tasted exactly like dirt. Then again, that could have been his cooking.

Scalious walked to the aquarium's simulated lakefront and went for a swim (just to make sure he still had it). He swam like a half-man, half-fish: he did human strokes, but moved extra quickly because of his webbed fingers and tail that swayed back and forth. Then he practiced climbing a display of fake trees to build his endurance and tested out the extra skin under his arms to see if he could fly. He had to use protective footwear because his feet weren't accustomed to the rough terrain—they were called "footie socks" and they had individual toe holes.

For the next few days, Professor Scalious did daily climbing drills after yoga, yelling, "One, Two! One, Two!" On his first attempt to climb the tree, he fell a few times because the suction cups on his fingers were dry and crusted from never using them before. But after a while, he could use the suction under his fingers to get a grip on the bark, and he zoomed up the tree as fast as a cheetah. He also practiced  swinging from tree to tree using his tongue to stick to things.

After his drills, Scalious began to pack. He packed some extra eyeglasses, a tiny lab coat, and a waterproof lab coat in case it ever rained while he was doing experiments. He brought along a notepad and a giant pen so he could take notes about the outside world. He also knew he had to brush up on his English because there weren't very many creatures around for him to talk to underneath his plastic rock. When he was practicing jumping off of shelves in the gift shop, a dictionary accidentally landed on him, so he used it as a study guide. His favorite words were "laboratory" and "hypothesis."

He also worked on other skills. For example, he knew he'd need to work on his camouflage so he could hide from his predators. One camouflage idea involved hiding under leaves and covering himself with mud, but not rocks, because that might weigh him down.

When he was done preparing for the trip, Professor Scalious was excited that he was about to leave his routine life. He still felt a little torn between leaving and staying—like he was about to be the new kid in school.

....

Over time, Ophelia began to fit in a little more at her high school. She was a genius, after all, and she knew from all her nonfiction nature reading just how to blend in to a new habitat. After carefully studying her surroundings—and her older sister—she developed a list of methods that would make her seem like one of the strange creatures she went to class with. The species was called teenagers.

....

HOW TO PRETEND YOU'RE A HIGH SCHOOLER:
A Guide by Ophelia

CARLOS DIAZ, ROXOLANA KRONSHTAL, AND ALIEZA RENTERIA, GRADE 4

Are you surrounded by teenagers? Do you have to go to high school? Use these quick tips to pretend you are a high schooler:

- Wear contacts and maybe a wig.
- Act really mature like a grownup.
- Talk in a deep voice.
- Dress up in cool, raw clothes with designs on them.
- Wear stylish gym shoes like Nikes or Jordans. Or wear high heels to make yourself look taller.

- Make the "Puppy Face" at your mom so she will give you money to go shopping.
- Carry a purse on your arm and wear earrings—have your mom help you put them on.
- When it's time for lunch, eat at a cool table and talk to your friends.
- When it's time for recess or time to go outside, don't look like you're having any fun.
- When you talk, say cool things like, "What's up?!" But only to your friends—not your teacher.
- Don't be weak or selfish.
- In class, put your hand on your head to look like you're bored, but secretly be smart and don't cheat. Study and don't talk in class.

- Pretend you can drive a car.
- Learn how to text and call people on phones that have keyboards. If you don't have a cell phone, use cardboard, paint, and stickers to make a fake one. Make the phone look like a "Touch Slide." It should be as big as a king-sized Kit Kat.
- Walk in school while texting or talking on your phone. Pretend to text your BFF and learn to use short phrases like OMG, G2G, and LOL.
- Use a pen because high schoolers think pencils are dorky.
- Know how to dance to whatever music a DJ or your friends are going to put on, or else you will look ridiculous. You

should be ready to dance to: Spanish music, hip hop, the Cha-Cha Slide, and the Cupid Shuffle. You can learn this from dance videos.

- On your way to your locker, only walk in the middle of the hallway, like you are a king or a queen. Walking in the middle of the hallway shows you are cool, not scared—you are popular. Little kids will step aside like you're walking on the red carpet—except it's a white floor. They see you coming.

Keep doing all these steps and no one will know you're not a real teen.

....

Sam was somewhat cheered up by his newly-discovered talent and the fun he had on the island with Venus. He began to like school a bit more each day, even without the help of his good friend Ophelia. But there was still one problem that he couldn't seem to shake.

....

SAM VS. THE SPROUTS:
A Journal Entry by Sam

JOWAN MACON, GRADE 8
....

It all started two days after the move. My parents recently started a little farm in the backyard. It looks like a green field with yellow spots. Makes me want to hurl. Venus would probably eat it. I never really cared about vegetables, but Brussels sprouts—eww, I hate 'em. My mom makes everything possible with the sprouts. Brussels on the cob especially. And the rest? You don't wanna go there.

At the dinner table, it's me, Ma, and Pa, with little Venus right under me. Brussels on the cob again. Somehow, Venus loves it. I give her some of mine. I never know why, but she belches and it smells like a Chicago hot dog stand where the real meat is. Boy, if only I could sneak away, I would go get some meat. Instead, I'm sitting here at a bogus table with this nasty food. Maybe Venus's hairballs would taste better than this.

"You know, you shouldn't feed Venus this," Ma says.

"Yeah, you need strong bones, Squirt," says Pa.

"Pa. That's milk. Besides, you know I hate Brussels sprouts like mom hates it when you spray your smelly cologne and hug her." Ma gets a weird look in her eye and Pa says, "I think we've heard enough. That's it! You and Venus go up to your room and think about what you did!"

Now, pause — I want to throw food at Pa, but if I do, Venus would eat it off of him.

"Yeah," I say instead. "I'll be thinking about something, all right..."

So Venus and I are in my room and I am trying to decide what to do with the sprouts. I am tossing Venus a ball of yarn and she is trying to catch it. Her head is going up and down, up and down. It's making her dizzy. And in a quick hurry, Venus jumps because she hears my loud voice saying, "I got it! I'll just pull them up every night and toss them in the lake."

This is a great idea.

So that night I'm staring the Brussels sprouts down, and they won't blink. I try to hold my eyelids up but I'm going to lose the water in my eyes. Three rows of five Brussels sprouts. Each time I pull one out, a little tick goes off in my head. Maybe my thoughts are trying to tell me something.

"I'm finished, and boy, does my back hurt," I think as I slap the sprouts in a rusty brown wheelbarrow.

"Whoosh!" All go in the water. I think I'm safe, for now.

The next morning I have a good feeling. "What's for breakfast?" I yell happily. Mom comes to the table with green pancake sprouts and a side of regular Brussels sprouts. They look like something you would find in a sewer, only they're cooked.

In my mind, I think I pulled them all up, but they must have grown back. The smart side says, "Ya think?! And I am trapped inside a doofus body."

I rush toward the window. There it is—fifteen horrors. Man, if only, if only I was on my island. That's the story of my life. My cat Venus is excited, but I'm so furious I quickly toss the whole plate on the floor. Venus runs up and dives in.

The morning comes again. I have no idea what Ma will make. And then on my plate sits eggsprouts — something like egg salad. This time I collapse on the floor. Venus collapses in my chair and takes a bite of the eggsprouts. I run to my room and Ma comes and asks, "What's wrong?"

"Everything," I say. "With the sprouts. Get rid of the pancake sprouts, the eggsprouts salad, and the Brussels on the cob. But keep the chicken sprouts and the sprouts sandwich. Also, I really want some ham."

Mom respectfully agrees with my idea. She says, "You have a choice of what to eat now."

"Yes!" someone says. But I didn't say anything—it was Pa. He secretly hated the sprouts, too!

That night, dinner smells so good. Mom makes a great ham. It's so brown and so hot, just like I like it. I give Venus some sprouts. She refuses after what happened with the eggsprouts, so I give her some ham, and in one lick she eats everything.

Then Mom announces, "Since there are no more sprouts, I have to make black-eyed peas."

"The singers?" I said.

"No, the peas."

I take a gasp and look at Pa as we shout, "NOOOOOOOOOOOOOOOOOO!!!!"

HE THOUGHT HE WOULD GO FOR IT

STORM JACKSON, GRADE 3

When Professor Scalious woke up, the first thing he saw was a calendar that said today was the day he would dig a tunnel to China and escape from the aquarium. He thought that would be a good place to start an adventure because he imagined the dirt was softer there than it was in Wisconsin. He wasn't totally sure about this but he imagined it and thought it sounded good.

The professor felt happy about his trip. He was on the excited side but he thought that if there were going to be a lot of people when he got there he would be nervous. For a minute, he scared himself by imagining new people saying, "What is that lizard thing? Ugh!" But he still thought he would go for it.

The first thing he did was finish packing for his trip. He brought his supplies from the gift shop and also a fake moustache so people wouldn't recognize him. He also packed some eye contacts so he could see better in the tunnel and not bump into people. He took his children's atlas, his diary, and his clothes. And he took the picture of his family to remember them.

Next, he went to have breakfast. Since he'd been so busy planning, he'd forgotten to eat for three days. Professor Scalious knew it was important to eat before his big trip because he didn't know how long it would take. He thought the trip might take six days. He thought, "That is way too long not to eat!"

Professor Scalious decided to have dirt for breakfast. He figured that he should get used to eating dirt, because it was all around him, and he might need to eat it in the tunnel when it was all that was there. Also, the bugs in the his refrigerator were so old that every time he opened it he would faint. He thought he would have only a small piece of dirt for breakfast, because he didn't want to make a big hole in his

house in case it rained or there was a blizzard while he was gone. He didn't want to come home to a mess as soon as he opened the door.

Professor Scalious made a machine to take care of his rock-house while he was gone. He programmed it to clean the house and water his plants—even the weeds—and make sure that if someone came up to the house to borrow his clothes they would not take EVERYTHING, even though they could take a few things.

"Robot, you better make sure nobody comes in my rock!" Professor Scalious warned the machine.

When he finished tidying up his rock-house, he clapped his hands together and cried, "Okay, here we go. Let me get my digging gloves on."

But it wasn't that easy. As soon as Professor Scalious put his wrinkly lizard hands into the ground, he had trouble digging. The ground was like concrete! His gloves were already ripped and when he took them off, his hands were all red and beating like a heart going "B-boom, b-boom, b-boom!"

"This is a problem," he said.

Professor Scalious went back home and made some space in his suitcase by pulling out sixty other pairs of gloves. He put them all on, because he hoped this way the gloves wouldn't rip. His hands looked like puffy pink layers of insulation, but it worked! He asked his robot machine to take him back to the place where he was starting his tunnel because it was just too much for one lizard to do.

When he began to dig, Professor Scalious was able to get through the dirt and he was surprised by what he saw. When he made the tunnel big enough, there were all sorts of soft hanging rocks and dirt above him. "Oh," he said. "More breakfast!"

Professor Scalious was using everything he had to dig. He was digging with his gloves. He was digging with his feet. He was even digging with his tail! But even with the gloves working, it was still hard. He went through his tunnel and didn't travel more than a block before he was tired.

"Whooo!" he said. "That was a lot of digging."

By now it was already 11 o'clock at night and Professor Scalious usually went to bed by 7:30 p.m. He was looking all messed up—dirt in his fake moustache (which was white, so the dirt really showed), and his clothes looking like the mud had attacked him. He had been digging and running from loose rocks all day. Suddenly he heard a strange *whoooooshing* noise. It was water from underground! It was coming toward him as fast as the speed of sound!

"No! Not to me! Please!" he yelled in an astonished voice. "I'm too old to die!"

Professor Scalious turned to run and tripped on a big rock. He did six flips right into the mud. He landed with a *whhhhsssbooom* and mud washed over him in a big wave.

"Enough's enough!" Professor Scalious yelled. "I hate mud! And I'm going back home to my rock!"

As soon as Professor Scalious got home and closed the door, he turned around and fell over. He was so tired he looked like an old rat, and he felt like his heart was beating and his muscles were already so stiff they wouldn't move.

He said to himself, "I'm so tired. I can't do it today. Maybe I'll do it next weekend."

He knew he'd have to find a different way.

. . . .

Sam realized that, try though he might, there would really be no getting away from those dreadful Brussels sprouts for long. He knew he'd have to keep working on his parents, but in the meantime he was going to have to come up with another way to avoid their revolting taste. After a couple of test-runs in the kitchen, he came up with a few good ideas.

. . . .

HOW TO COVER UP THE TASTE OF BRUSSELS SPROUTS:
Two Sure-Fire Methods

ANJELINA JOLEEN JIMENEZ AND LESLIE D. SADKOWSKI, GRADE 4

There are two ways to cover up the taste of Brussels sprouts.

Method I:

First, take a Brussels sprout, a piece of chocolate, a toothpick, and a knife. Next, wash the Brussels sprout with water. Then, dry it with a paper towel. Cut the Brussels sprout in half with the knife. Take the chocolate and cut it with the knife, but only cut a little piece. Now, drop the chocolate in the sprout and close the two halves of the sprout. After that, take the toothpick and stick it through the sprout. And that's how you cover up the terrible taste of Brussels sprouts.

Method 2:

First, get Brussels sprouts. Second, cook the Brussels sprouts and get seasoning. Then, stir the Brussels sprouts and put a lid on the pan. Next, heat up a tortilla and make it into a taco. You can add tomato and lettuce. You will not be able to taste the Brussels sprouts at all!

In school, Sam's class was working on persuasive writing. When it came time for their big essay assignment, he knew just what his topic would be...

WHY BRUSSELS SPROUTS ARE BAD FOR YOU:
An Essay by Sam

MARTA MARCZUK, GRADE 7

Did you look down at your plate and see a big bunch of Brussels sprouts? Don't you think that you shouldn't eat them? I have done much research and I have a lot of proof of why Brussels sprouts are bad. Some of my conclusions on what they do to you are: They stop you from growing taller, they make you sick, and you become as big and round as a Brussels sprout.

You shouldn't eat Brussels sprouts because they make you stop growing taller. According to my research, a study was conducted in 1995 by a Professor Scalious at the University of Avian. He gave one person only Brussels sprouts to eat for a whole year while the other person ate anything **but** Brussels sprouts. At the end of the year, the person who ate the Brussels sprouts was still five feet tall and the other person grew to six feet! It was all over the news and in the newspapers throughout the whole world: don't eat Brussels sprouts.

You shouldn't eat Brussels sprouts because they make you sick. A kid from my class came to school saying he ate a bucket of Brussels sprouts for breakfast. To me, he looked a bit green and he had an odd expression on his face. A minute later, he ran to the office claiming he had a huge headache. He had gone blind and had

a sore throat. When they went to the doctor, he said it was caused by the Brussels sprouts, and the kid got a terrible disease from them called Bruspro disease. He couldn't go to school for a month! Now he can't even look at Brussels sprouts. Of course, the doctor said not every Brussels sprout has the disease, but there is a big chance you might get it. I don't think you'd like to try.

You shouldn't eat Brussels sprouts because a single Brussels sprout can make you as round and big as a sprout. One day, I refused to eat Brussels sprouts at dinner. As a punishment, the next day I had to eat them all day long. When I woke up the next morning I couldn't get through the door! When I put on my shirt, all the buttons popped off. I couldn't get my pants higher than my knees, and my hand was so huge that I couldn't brush my teeth. When I finally got out the door, I rolled down the stairs and I couldn't hug my mom because my round body was blocking my hands. Of course, my parents didn't believe that it was the Brussels sprouts' fault, and they kept feeding me Brussels sprouts. Now I have the nickname of Brussels Ball. Do you want to be in my place? Probably not.

Yet there are people who think Brussels sprouts are healthy. Are they healthy when they make you blind, round, and stunt your growth? No — so don't eat Brussels sprouts.

So are you still looking down at those Brussels sprouts? Don't worry. Your mother won't notice if you move them around and say you're done. And if she still makes you eat them, don't worry. I am starting an Anti-Brussels Campaign. Just contact me at my Brussels sprouts farm and sign a petition. If you do all those things you will never have to eat them again! Don't ever be round, blind, and the same short height again. Say no to Brussels sprouts!

....

Still discouraged from his last attempt to flee the aquarium, Professor Scalious was beginning to think he'd never see anything but the inside of his plastic rock. But just when he'd resigned himself to a lifetime of staring at the well-worn halls of the aquarium, Professor Scalious had a brilliant stroke of luck.

....

GOING TO L.A.

JOEL ORTIZ, GRADE 5
....

Professor Scalious sat in his rock-house in Wisconsin Blue Aquarium, watching his hometown Bucks with his daily lottery ticket in his hand. He was feeling bad because he hadn't gotten to finish the tunnel.

"I can't believe I did so much work for nothing," he thought to himself.

During a timeout, a commercial came on:

"Hello, this is your chance to win $5,000 and a trip to Los Angeles, California! The numbers are 8, 26, 52, 12, 1, 5!"

Professor Scalious looked at his ticket and was so shocked he conducted a heart test with a special wire he had invented. His numbers were the winning numbers!

"WAKABULIA! I'm going to L.A.!" said the professor. He was excited because he would go to the Worldwide Science Fair and would buy Book Two of *The Explanatory Guide Toward the Studies of Chemistry.*

Professor Scalious borrowed Aunt Mary's dune buggy and finally—*finally*—left the aquarium. He drove as fast as he could to the MLC—Milwaukee Lottery Center. But he was shocked when he claimed his prize.

"Listen, bub. You're a lizard," said the clerk. "Show me your ticket."

He brought his ticket and got his prize.

"Bub, you're scheduled for March 18. United flight 127. Row 1, seat BC."

Professor Scalious jumped into his car, but went 62 miles per hour in a 15 mph zone, so he got a $50 fine. He had $4,950 left. He did the Moonwalk Shuffle—his dance made up for celebration.

"I'm going to L.A.! I'm going to L.A.! WOO! Look at me!"

His only problem was that his flight left at 1:00 a.m., and it was 3:00 p.m.! Professor Scalious was so happy, he did not see that his flight was in a few hours. He packed up and went to the airport. As he entered, he heard:

"Welcome to Milwaukee International Airport. ALL animals travel in the luggage cabin."

He began to worry, "Oh, my gosh! I'm going to be thrown around!"

When he arrived at the passport showing, the security guard said, "Professor Stephen Scalious, come this way."

The guard led him to an airplane. The time was 12:59 a.m., and Professor Scalious was shocked to find no one else onboard the airplane. He had his own plane! On his flight, he had a TV, video games, music, and much food. But he went straight toward the books.

"*World War II, Kobe Bryant,* ah ha! *The Explanatory Guide Toward the Studies of Chemistry!*"

When he got to L.A. and left the airport, the professor looked for a hotel, but only the zoo let him in. His room was near the exotic animals, and he was frightened by the lion.

"Hey! You scared me, big fella!"

Professor Scalious hailed a taxi and drove off to the Staples Center for the Worldwide Science Fair. The arena was very crowded, and he was the only lizard. The professor tried to avoid being stepped on, and he trotted over to the chemistry section. He was finally able to meet Dr. James Jackson, author of *The Explanatory Guide Toward the Studies of Chemistry*. Dr. Jackson was 6'7" and only 25 years old.

Both of them immediately got engaged in conversation.

"Oh my! Dr. James Jackson! I can't believe it!" exclaimed Professor Scalious.

"Pleased to meet you! Happy to have another fellow follower!" said Dr. Jackson.

"Doctor, I have to ask. Where can I buy Book Two of *The*

Explanatory Guide Toward the Studies of Chemistry?"

Dr. James Jackson paused. He whispered, "I only have two copies. The book is not yet in stores."

"Oh," said Professor Scalious, disappointed.

Professor Scalious told him about himself.

Dr. Jackson was moved.

"I am a local scientist. I would not be here if it was not for luck."

Dr. Jackson frowned, a tear welling in his eye.

"Well, come over to my lab tonight. I'll give you a copy of the book."

"Thank you! Thank you!" said Professor Scalious. He left the Staples Center, but on his way out, he spotted an ad. It read: LAKERS VS. BUCKS – TOMORROW – LOWER LEVEL SUITES FOR $40.

Professor Scalious stepped over to buy a ticket. He put the ticket in his pocket and found his airplane ticket stub. Shocked, he saw it said: ONE-WAY TICKET – MILWAUKEE TO LOS ANGELES.

His knees wobbled and he got lightheaded. He woke up two hours later in the vet's office. The vet was filing a report. Professor Scalious saw the doctor write, "Talking lizard faints in Staples Center."

Professor Scalious looked at the vet, a young, muscular guy. His room had red walls and very intricate tile. Professor Scalious talked with the vet and found out where he could buy an airplane ticket, which was right next door.

After a long argument, and a small fight, Professor Scalious got a ticket for departure in two days. He remembered the visit to Dr. Jackson's lab, and went there next. The lab was a huge mansion lab in Hollywood.

Professor Scalious knocked on the door and a small child answered.

"Daddy, a lizard knocked on the door. Can I eat it?"

A voice answered, "No!"

Dr. Jackson approached the door.

"Hey, Professor Scalious! Come on in!"

Professor Scalious was led to the lab. Dr. Jackson had a very nice house. The walls were beautiful and there were stairs and pieces of rare art. They went into the laboratory.

"Here, you can have this." Dr. Jackson gave Professor Scalious a copy of Book Two of *The Explanatory Guide Toward the Studies of Chemistry*.

"Thank you very much!" said Professor Scalious.

They talked sciency stuff and Professor walked away with a book, and many parts for the machine he was planning to build. Two days later, Professor Scalious was driven to the airport, and as he arrived in Milwaukee, he exclaimed, "Home, sweet home."

HOW TO BUILD A DRISUB®

SETH CORPUZ, GRADE 6

Professor Scalious couldn't wait go travelling again. But there was a still the problem: Unless he was going to win another vacation, he couldn't get out of the plastic rock.

Professor Scalious felt sad his tunnel idea hadn't worked. He was as sad as an abandoned dog. Suddenly, a book from his bookshelf fell and hit him on the head. The book was about drills and submarines. It was called *How to Build a DriSub®*. Then an idea hit him. He is just going to invent something—a submarine with a drill in front of it!

Professor Scalious used his bookshelf to build the DriSub® (which was short for "Dry Submarine"). He used a sharp rock to carve pieces of the machine and mud to put it together.

The DriSub® was as big as a man's shoe. It was brown and had a big window in the front so he could see where he was going. It also had a big drill in the front with two hands to help dig. When it drilled, it would sound like a dog barking.

Professor Scalious used his old skin as fuel for the DriSub®. Then, he opened the hatch and went in. He sat on the seat and fastened his seatbelt and pushed the bright red button to turn the DriSub® ON.

Then he told himself, "This might not work." But he tried it anyway.

The DriSub® worked super-well! Professor Scalious was yelling with joy. The drill started to spin and pierced into the wall. Rocks flew everywhere, the hands started to dig, and the sound of the DriSub® started to make the dog-barking sound. He was ready to begin his journey—this time, for real!

SCALIOUS DIGS THE TUNNEL

JENNIFER SORIA, GRADE 5

The next morning, Professor Scalious grabbed a jar of bugs that he kept for snacks and his bug-shaped pillow that comforted him, and he got in the submarine through a hole at the top. He was anxious because he had wanted to accomplish this for so long in his life, and now was so close. In the blink of an eye, he was digging.

Professor Scalious turned on the submarine and this time he

thought it sounded like a car engine. He turned the light to see where he was going.

Then the light inside started to fail, and as Professor Scalious dug he heard eerie noises he'd never heard before. He started to get scared.

All he could see in the tunnel were creatures he'd never seen before, digging in the dirt. In his window he saw a mole. He tried to go backward, but realized he'd forgotten to make his submarine able to go back. Professor Scalious decided to ask the mole for help finding a light. The mole tried to explain but since the mole was eating worms Professor Scalious couldn't understand him.

Professor Scalious tried to get the mole to eat faster, and finally the mole told Professor Scalious to follow him toward the light. Professor Scalious invited the mole into the submarine so he wouldn't be lonely. They went along the tunnel and found some treasures along the way. As they finally got closer to the end, Professor Scalious yelled "Yippee!" and headed toward the light.

....

The Bookie wasn't Ophelia's only invention. When she wasn't busy with high school or working at the bakery or helping around the house, Ophelia spent all her time working on new creations. She figured she'd made too many to count. Here are just a few of her favorites...

....

THE PIZZACHRON 3000 AND THE SECRET TV 1000

JADALYNNE GAGO-IZQUIERDO, GRADE 2

Once Ophelia made a great invention. She named it the Pizzachron 3000. It made pizzas all day long! The specialty was pepperoni sausage. It was cheesy and gooey and it had super delicious tomato sauce and there was scrumptious yummy pepperoni and sausage.

The Pizzachron 3000 had a button you could push, and Ophelia and her siblings could form an assembly line when they ran it. It started with little plates with two kinds of sauces: regular sauce and hot sauce. In the Pizzachron 3000, you could have any ingredient, like shrimp or seaweed or sardines. You could even have a tower of stacked pepperoni pizzas three feet high! Or you could have lots and lots of cheese, like "monsterella" cheese! It was not a monster. You couldn't have weird cheese like Gruyere or Brie.

Then Ophelia made another invention. She called it the Secret

TV 1000. You could watch TV in school without teachers seeing it. You needed glasses to see the secret TV. Ophelia did have glasses, but she had sunglasses because she was in summer school when she invented it. In the winter she wore contacts so that she could see her secret TV. She liked to watch *Elmo* best, and *Miss BG*, who was from Cuba! But her really favorite show was *Alfred the Hedgehog*, because it had mysteries.

FIFI: THE HOUSEWORK/ HOMEWORK ROBOT

ANDRENIQUE PATTERSON, GRADE 6

Ophelia's robot was designed to help with both housework and homework. The robot was gray and about 4 feet tall. It had long arms and feet that it could roll on and a door on its back that you could open. It talked in a voice that had an echo to it. Ophelia came up with the

idea because she and her mother needed help taking care of the house and her seven brothers and sisters. In order to make the robot, Ophelia did a lot of research on how robots were built. She drew plans and pictures of the robot before she started building it. Then she asked some people at school for help. Her

teachers told her what they knew about building, and she told them how she wanted the robot to come out and what she wanted it to do.

The robot picked up clothes and washed them. It also helped Ophelia and her brothers and sisters do their homework. The robot was especially good at math and science, but it was hard for the robot to do writing—it just couldn't write the way a human can. In the morning the robot walked Ophelia to school, but it didn't go inside. It just left her there.

The robot's name was Fifi. Ophelia's family liked the robot, and her brothers and sisters asked if it could come out to play. Fifi was only allowed to play outside if Ophelia was right there to watch her brothers and sisters, because she was afraid they might break the robot. Fifi could play hide and seek and run races against Ophelia's brothers and sisters. Fifi was happy to be part of a nice family.

THE MAGICAL CRAYON MACHINE

DIOVIONE HARRIS, GRADE 4

Ophelia created a crayon machine because her mom would never buy her crayons, so she thought of something and said, "Wow! How about I make a crayon machine?"

The crayon machine Ophelia made was blue, white, and pink, and it had a clear top on it. The way it worked was you put four different paint colors in four slots. If you said "Blue!" a blue crayon

would pop out, and if you said "Pink!" a pink crayon would pop out, and so on. You would fill up the slots with any paint colors you were going to use that day.

The name of Ophelia's invention was the Magical Crayon Machine. Ophelia invented it so she could sell some crayons and keep others for herself. Ophelia thought this would be a great invention because

nobody had ever invented a crayon machine. The crayon machine was really big—so big she had to stand on a chair to put the paint in.

Ophelia made this crayon machine to impress her mother, and also so she wouldn't have to ask her mother to buy her crayons when she needed them. When Ophelia made the crayon machine, her mom thought she was extra smart, and started letting Ophelia go outside more. Then Ophelia went to school and started telling everybody about it. They did not believe her and said, "Bring it to school." But the crayon machine was too big and heavy to move, so they came to her house to look at it instead. Her teacher thought it was cool.

THE DISHWASHING DING MACHINE

EVA BERNATEK, GRADE 2

Ophelia had too much work because she had to wash the dishes for her whole family. She thought this was boring and she had lots of other things to do, like drying the dishes, doing her homework, cooking for her whole family, inventing things, and playing with her brothers and sisters when she had to. To solve this problem, she invented the Dishwashing Ding Machine. It was big and square and had sticks and spoons sticking out.

The machine took a dish and wiped it clean. Ophelia would put the dish in and they went down a slide. Water and soap came on and sprayed them, and a cloth came out to wipe the dishes clean. Then another part grabbed the dishes and put them in the right spot. The clean and dirty water went into a bucket, which went into the sink and then the sink got washed so it wasn't messy. Her family thought it was no good until she showed them how it worked and then they liked it.

MICHAEL, THE ICE CREAM ROBOT

JAMELL RICHARDSON, GRADE 2

Ophelia invented Michael, the Ice Cream Robot, because she was lonely and she wanted ice cream. Ophelia liked ice cream as much as candy and a birthday party together. She also liked

robots. She invented Michael so she could eat ice cream whenever she wanted, because normally her parents wouldn't let her—Michael could make ice cream in the shape of healthy food to trick them.

All of Ophelia's brothers and sisters wanted Michael, and Ophelia thought they were going to take him, but then Michael made them the best ice cream ever and they forgot about it. He made sour and sweet flavors with a cherry on top. Ophelia's favorite flavor was Rainbow Sherbet.

Michael also caught fish because Ophelia liked to go fishing. She made Michael for her birthday and then Michael made her an ice cream birthday cake. Ophelia and her robot ended up being friends, because Michael did a lot of nice things for her and they spent a lot of time together.

As Professor Scalious travelled around the world, tunneling from place to place in his beloved DriSub®, he found himself inspired to write about his new experiences.

THE MOUNTAIN:
A Poem by Professor Stephen Scalious

HILDA VILLA, GRADE 5

somewhere in the ice mountains,
professor scalious looks up at the peaks covered
with white snow. He plants his hiking sticks.
The ice and snow are hard
as a concrete wall.
He pulls himself up to start the adventure.
He breathes the wind
through his blue scarf and gloves and slow dances
with the branches of the trees.
icicles tinkle together like many glass bottles.
He approaches the first peak and jumps
with excitement.
He builds a small fire from boney twigs
and crunchy leaves. shivering, he melts
snow into boiling water.
It warms him up like a baby
crawling for the first time.
professor scalious closes his eyes
and smiles.

A JOURNAL ENTRY BY PROFESSOR STEPHEN SCALIOUS

ANGEL ROJAS, GRADE 3

Hello, i'm professor Stephen Scalious and i love to travel because there wasn't anything to do in Wisconsin. i also like to travel because i meet new friends and animals in all sorts of new places.

i carry around a children's atlas. it smells like different

foods and spices because it has pictures of different spices and maps where you can buy them. it also has information about how different animals from different countries make spices. i'd like to find the animals so i can keep them as pets and study them and show them to my friends. i've travelled a lot of places. Today, i'm travelling to the jungle and finding different animals.

Did i tell you that i'm an amateur scientist, too? maybe i didn't. ok, let's stop talking about that and talk about my travels. i want to find animals like jaguars with black and red stripes and snakes with yellow polka-dots, but i'm scared of spiders and i hope i don't see any in the jungle. okay, i've got to go — my submarine is running!

PROFESSOR SCALIOUS'S SOCCER ADVENTURE

MALIK BROWN, GRADE 7

Professor Stephen Scalious got interested in soccer when he was crawling down the street on one of his travels and saw a huge TV with people playing soccer on it. He fell in love with soccer when he saw a soccer player named Mesut Ozil doing bicycle kicks, which is when the ball is in the air and the person in the air sort of does a backflip and hits the ball with the top of his foot. Professor Scalious had always imagined that his long-lost father was a soccer player, so he had confidence that he could play well, and tried to do the bicycle kick, too. He almost made it, but the ball was really high, and Professor Scalious was too small, so he flipped but didn't reach the ball.

He decided he would head to Germany and go to Oktoberfest so he could play soccer with other lizards. He tunneled there and hopped out on a beach. Just then, he saw a huge fish head at the beach and he was scared because that could only mean one thing— German lizards. They loved to eat fish bodies.

"Holy Mackerel!" Professor Scalious said to himself. "I bet the lizards here are twice the size of me. I can imagine them already: big and scary, but good looking. It doesn't matter—I will not be a chicken. I am Professor Scalious."

Just then Professor Scalious saw some lizards approaching on the beach, and to his surprise, he met some old friends he had grown up with in Wisconsin! They had gone to Germany fifteen years ago for Oktoberfest and he hadn't seen them since then.

"Jerry and Tania! Oh my gosh! Long time, no see!' said Professor Scalious.

"I know. Fifteen years, man. I missed ya!" said Tania.

" 'Sup, Professor Scale!" said Jerry.

"So...why are you here?" proclaimed Professor Scalious.

"To watch a team called XLSV go against some other team sponsored by Oktoberfest," said Jerry.

"XLSV—is that Xtra Lazy Sad Vipers?" asked Professor Scalious.

"No, silly, it stands for Xcellent Lizards, Scary Vampires," said Tania, giggling at the same time.

"Oh," said Professor Scalious, hesitating.

Professor Scalious thought about how he had messed up the bicycle kick in front of Mesut Ozil. He wanted to do better, and

had an idea. "Hey, I think we should be the other team. What do you say you and I get some other players together and go up against XLSV?"

XLSV vs Lizards: the game was fast, then got slow. During the game, Professor Scalious was attacker. Jerry and Tania were midfielders. The game started and Professor Scalious made two goals. He was showing off, doing the Worm and acting like a fish getting out of the water. The game was over and the lizards won the game 2-0. Professor Scalious was so happy he said, "We won! We beat those sad vipers!"

Everyone started laughing and cheering. Professor Scalious loved the game so much he created a time-travel capsule so they could go back in time and beat XLSV again. When they began to play, Professor Scalious said, "Come on, you're gonna lose again, suckers!" But as he was saying this, they lost the game. Everyone started cheering and shouting for XLSV. Professor Scalious was so devastated he kicked the time capsule and dislocated his foot. Then he went back to the beach and used his underground power drill to go back to Wisconsin.

Just as he got inside his plastic rock-house, he got a phone call from Germany.

"Hello," he said.

"Yeah, Scalious? This is Jerry. Um, bro, you left your time capsule and XLSV is using it, trying to break it."

"Oh, *snap*," said Professor Scalious. He hung up the phone and used his jet pack to get to Germany. He was a little scared about flying it there but he didn't want anyone else to lie and say they made the invention.

When he made it there, he first went to a German kabob place made with fish and alligators. He loved this food because his Aunt Mary used to cook it for him when he was little. After he ate, he ran around town looking for his time capsule, but it was nowhere to be found.

He texted Jerry—WHERE IS THE TIME CAPSULE? But Jerry didn't reply.

Next, he called Tania. Tania answered but she was screaming and he couldn't understand her. Professor Scalious kept yelling "Tania?!" but she hung up. Scalious kept looking until he only had one place left: the Oktoberfest building. So he ran there and went inside. It was pitch black. Professor Scalious was looking for the light switch when, all of a sudden, the light went on and he saw all the lizards with party hats yelling "Surprise!"

Professor Scalious was flabbergasted. He told them, "I'm running all around town looking for my time capsule, and you guys pulled this prank on me." But after he said that, he became really happy and enjoyed the party with his friends.

Most of the time, Ophelia's new inventions were successful, but you can't win them all. In her long career of inventions, a few of them didn't work out as planned. Here are a few of the contraptions she filed under "NEEDS-SOME-TWEAKING INVENTIONS":

THE WATER GENERATOR 2000

ARIANA SALGADO, GRADE 2

Ophelia's fear of being thirsty made her invent the Water Generator 2000. With this invention she would never be thirsty—

wherever she was, she could always get a cup of water. It could make four flavors: strawberry, raspberry, cranberry, and banana. The flavors were her favorites and the favorites of her brothers and sisters. Ophelia added them so she didn't always have to drink plain water. The machine could make bubbly, carbonated water, too. It could also make ice cubes and straws, and it could make the drinks a little fancy. The generator looked like a regular remote. It was gray, rectangular, and had eight buttons. There was a button for each of the flavors and also a PLAIN button, a BUBBLY button, a FANCY button, and the ON/OFF button. Once, Ophelia tripped on the remote and accidentally hit the ON button. The Water Generator 2000 sprung a leak and started leaking all the colors and all kinds of water.

THE SLINGSHOT

MARC MENDEZ, GRADE 2

Ophelia wanted to play football because she saw the Bears play on TV and it looked fun. She got tired of running around by herself, so she created the Slingshot. It was a football-throwing invention that looked like a giant slingshot, and it helped by throwing a football for her and catching the ball like a receiver. Her teacher thought it was cool and other kids at school wanted to use it for practice. The problem with the Slingshot was that sometimes it would keep running away with the ball, or sometimes it would throw

the footballs so far that they flew out of the field, where they would get lost or cause car accidents. Ophelia fixed the invention so it would throw the ball slower and lower.

Another problem with the Slingshot was that in the winter, it froze in place and couldn't throw footballs anymore. Ophelia fixed this by moving the Slingshot into her kitchen. She turned on her oven and put the Slingshot in front of it so it would melt. When it was unfrozen, they took the Slingshot back to the field, but then it would just get frozen again, so Ophelia had to keep taking it to her kitchen.

THE SPAGHETTI MACHINE

LEE KENDRICK, GRADE 2

Ophelia really liked spaghetti. In fact, she LOVED spaghetti! She decided she wanted to make only spaghetti for dinner. She used metal and the stove to make a Spaghetti Machine, which was kind of like a robot with arms. It made a "MEEP" robot sound when it made spaghetti. If it dropped something, its eyes opened wide and it said "EEE!" So it started dropping things.

First, it dropped the spaghetti and the hot water, and the hot

water went everywhere! It was splashing all over the kitchen! It took the sauce, opened it, and poured it on its face.

"Oh, yummy!" said the robot. Then it started saying "AHH!" and turned its face back and forth—it was pretty broken. Then it put its head in the water and it froze and fell over! Ophelia came in and found the robot.

She said, "Are you playing around?" Then she said, "I hate you, spaghetti robot!" And she walked away, leaving the robot in the kitchen. During the night, the robot came into her room and hugged her. But it was still not working right and so Ophelia made another robot. This one made pizza.

Meanwhile, the spaghetti-making robot blew up...Ophelia never saw it again! But one piece is still roaming around Chicago, trying to make spaghetti.

And where was Sam during all of this? Making new discoveries. On his island, at school, even in his Brussels sprouts field—though the biggest discovery there wouldn't come until later. Things were looking up. That is, until he made one discovery he would rather have avoided.

THE NOT SO GREAT ~~BOOGERDORK~~ BOOGLEDORF:
As Told by Sam

AMINE AHMEDYAHIA, GRADE 7

Finally, after a week of begging my mom to take me to the coffee shop called The Milk Store, she agreed to do so. It recently opened up and all my friends were talking about it and saying it was good. They said they even sell coffee pizza! At 8:29 p.m., my mom and I left for the coffee shop. In the car, all I did was dream about coffee pizzas.

When we got there, I found out all my friends lied to me. The Milk Store was crowded with old people and smelled like sweat. They didn't even sell coffee pizzas!

"Can we go home?" I asked.

"No, you've been begging to go here for a year!" My mom responded.

"Not a year — a week."

"Same thing. You're stuck here now and you have to deal with it." My mom gave me ten dollars and started toward the door.

"Where are you going?" I yelled.

"I'm late for work!"

"But you don't have work on Thurs—"

The coffee shop door closed behind my mom and cut off my sentence. I knew I wasn't going to stand up for forty-five minutes waiting for her, so I walked over to the counter.

"I would like some coffee, please!" I demanded.

"One cup of coffee for the gentleman in the blue shirt, coming right up!" said the man behind the counter.

I sat down next to an old man who was looking grouchy. He was mumbling facts to himself. This was really annoying, so I moved one chair to the right.

"Sluuuurp!"

Ugh.

"SLUUURP!" A louder annoying slurp. Great. I was stuck there for at least forty-one more minutes with a grouchy old man who slurped louder than anyone I've ever seen.

I walked up to the old man and scolded him as much as I could. I could tell he didn't care because instead of giving me an apology, he gave me a cake **in my face**.

"I've had enough of him! Listen, old man, you have got to stop! You either slurp quieter or get out of the coffee shop!" I spit out chunks of cake as I yelled.

"I am no old man! I am the great super-villain William Harold James Boogledorf III!" he screamed.

"I don't care who you are, Boogerdork."

"It's Boogledorf! And you'll never make me stop!" he screamed as he ran out the door.

I called my mom.

"Mom, I'm going to walk home."

"No, it's too dangerous!" she cried.

"We only live a mile away!"

"No!"

"But there was this weird Boogledorf guy. He threw cake at me, slurped his coffee really loud, and claimed to be a super-villain."

"Okay, fine," my mom responded, "but be careful."

I hung up the phone and headed home. On the way, I felt like someone was breathing down my neck and I heard boring, useless facts.

"Bread cost 14 cents in 1950!"

I turned and looked around, but found nobody. Then, another boring fact:

"I eat stamps for lunch and breakfast."

I turned around again and still found no one. I decided that I would just ignore everything. After ten minutes filled with ten boring facts, I finally made it home.

I went to sleep as soon as I got inside. When I woke up the next day, my room and every other room in my house was filled with cardboard. This must have been the doing of Boogledorf! I informed my mom about everything that happened at the coffee shop the day before. She called the police and told them everything she knew about Boogledorf. They didn't find any records of him. Either that, or they just didn't care.

Every day for a whole week, he sent hundreds of boxes to our house and my mom made me clean it up. That's pretty much how I spent winter break. I hated it, and hated Boogerdork, too.

Sam wasn't the only one whose life was suddenly filled with cardboard. While Sam was cleaning it out of his house, Ophelia was making inventions with it.

THE CARDBOARD COMPANY

BRIAN SAUCEDO, GRADE 5

Everyday, Ophelia walked to the cardboard company where she worked. Her parents had been warned that they would lose their house, because they were not paid well at work. So when

she finished high school at the age of ten, Ophelia found a job at the cardboard factory right by her house.

All day long, Ophelia sorted the pieces of cardboard by the materials they were made of. It was an underground factory and Ophelia liked it there. Sometimes it smelled like rats because they lived there and got in through holes.

Ophelia also made great inventions using the cardboard and some electricity, and her inventions worked. Ophelia made toys for her siblings. She made cars for her brothers and dolls that talked for her sisters. Ophelia mostly liked working at the company because she liked to work on her cardboard inventions, but there was only one problem: She got in trouble a lot for nothing, like when she took her five-minute break to read her new favorite book, *The Adventures of Professor Stephen Scalious*. Ophelia loved it because it had action and adventure. But when her boss saw her reading it, she got in trouble and she had to read a book called *Facts About Cardboard* instead, which Mr. Aggressive gave her. That's what Ophelia called her boss.

....

Meanwhile, Professor Scalious continued his travels...

....

IN THE RAINFOREST

LUCERO HERRERA, GRADE 5 ....

In the rainforest, Professor Scalious gazed at the big beautiful birds. The birds were like giant skyscrapers and were so colorful they seemed to be rainbows. Professor Scalious saw the large soggy

trees. They looked fifty times bigger than he was! He felt the moss on trees that felt like goo. The moss also smelled more terrible than his socks. His lunch was so tasty, Professor Scalious felt like a king. As he ate his fly sandwich, fly wings fell out of the bread. He listened to the birds singing beautifully and took pictures of the birds. The clicking of his camera was louder than the tapping of the rain.

NEW USES FOR CARDBOARD BOXES:
As Told by Ophelia

ZAKARIA CHIHAB, GRADE 7

Yesterday the manager at the cardboard factory was sick. He caught polka-dot flu from his neighbor's dog. He called us at the factory to tell us we have to come up with new types and uses for cardboard boxes and the deadline is today. The reason why the manager wanted us to come up with new ideas was because people were getting sick of the square-shaped box, and they're asking for new shapes and designs on the box.

Cardboard boxes are normally used to keep your stuff in, like a storage box, but I figured out some other uses. More creative ways a box could be used include wearing it as a hat, as a last resort to a costume party. You could also use it to keep your head dry from the rain. (Number of uses: 1.) Or you could sleep in a box. (Temporary use only. If you hate paying the mortgage, you could live in it fulltime.) You're also able to use a box to get something you're normally not able to reach. And you can cut

out a piece from the box to make a plane, but not a real plane. With a couple of boxes, you can make armor and run through the neighbor's lawn without fearing that wretched dog's growl.

In addition, you can use a box as a practice target. (Example: archery.) You can also use a box to structure a hamster cage, or to help you carry stuff upstairs. You can use a box as a sled or a boat—although you might sink.

This morning when I arrived at work, the manager was feeling better, especially after I told him about all the new box ideas. He congratulated me on my work. In fact, he threw a party in my honor! The party had a box-shaped cake, and I got to wear one of my box ideas (the last-resort hat). In fact, after everyone saw the hat, they all wanted one, too.

....

As Professor Scalious continued his travels around the world, he was mesmerized again and again by the new sights and sounds that surrounded him. As he recorded a final poem en route to Tennessee, he had no idea that the next place he popped up would be the most important of all.

....

ADVENTURE:
A Poem by Professor
Stephen Scalious

CHINA HILL, GRADE 8
....

Traveling, oh the joy it brings!
i always find beautiful things
to go far, or to go near,
everywhere, here and there,
as far as the moon—

it's terrible when the day ends soon.
it's always exciting when i open my door,
even to go as close as the store.
i hope to see more.

oceans to beaches,
lakes to rivers —
the world is one big oyster to me.
i go to the beach; it's my favorite place.
i love the sand until it gets on my face.

The sun is wonderful, but it is hot
and that i do not like a lot.

soon the sun goes to sleep
and i must crawl
back to my lab.

my laboratory is very cold
Everything inside looks dusty and old.
my time machine might be my greatest joy —

when i go back to my lab, i go to my time machine and visit
myself at the beach.

PART 3

A GREAT TEAM

GOPHERS!

JAMES ANDERSEN III, GRADE 3

On Sam's farm, there was a field and a barn. The Brussels sprouts field was as huge as a soccer field. The soil was brown and the Brussels sprouts were the size of golf balls. There was also a really tall red silo filled with bats and owls.

Sam's house was on the farm. It was a small, dark green house. Inside the house, there were stairs, windows, doors, and two bathrooms (one on the top floor, one on the bottom floor). There were two bedrooms: one for Sam and one for Sam's parents. The house had a room with a TV and a game cube, where he played games. There was nothing else interesting about the house. Sam liked to be in the house just about as much as he liked to be on the farm.

One day, Sam was inside the house playing video games. His father was out fertilizing the Brussels sprouts and he discovered the gophers one hour later. Then Sam came out to the field.

His father said, "Hey son! There are some gophers out here!" He was pretty angry. Sam had never seen him that angry before.

Sam said, "Don't get mad! Just get rid of them and put some traps out!"

So his father went to the general store and bought some traps. Sam and his father went out to the field and put out traps with Brussels sprouts inside. The gophers liked Brussels sprouts because they were vegetables and they were healthy. They also liked green stuff and other vegetables.

That night Sam and his parents went to the table and ate dinner.

Sam's dad said, "The gophers are out there and we need to get rid of them, but it is so difficult to get rid of them. There are too many of them—maybe 1,000 of them, and they keep on multiplying."

Sam said, "If the gophers like the Brussels sprouts, we have to share the stuff." Secretly, he cared about the gophers because they sometimes didn't have any food. Plus they got rid of the Brussels sprouts.

Then Sam's family turned on the TV while they ate the rest of their dinners. Overnight, the gophers went in the traps because it smelled better in there than in the fields and there was a trip plate in the traps. In the middle of the night, the gophers bumped the trip plate and the trapdoors closed. In the morning, Sam and his father found that one of the gophers had escaped. Sam felt happy for that gopher.

Then the gophers who were left in the traps played a trick on Sam's father. A few more of the gophers got out of the traps, because more of the traps had holes in them. Sam's father found the traps with the holes. Sam realized that there were too many holes in the traps and too many gophers were getting out. If the farm were going to stay in business for his parents, he'd have to take care to catch them next time.

NICE TO MEET YOU

KRISTINE MARISOL RIOS AND JONATHAN ANGEL MERCADO, GRADE 6

Sam was asleep in his bed dreaming about catching gophers when an annoying sound woke him up. A *munch, crunch, munch* was coming from somewhere outside under the tall grass. Sam immediately jumped up and ran down the stairs and tripped. Instead of worrying about his scratches, he got up quickly, concerned about what the gophers were doing to the Brussels sprouts.

Outside, he started to look for a gopher, but instead he found a purple-spotted lizard wearing a lab coat and eating Brussels sprouts. Sam ran to grab the lizard right away. Sam trapped it and picked it up.

"Hi. Where am I?" the lizard asked. Sam dropped the lizard, surprised it could talk.

"That's not a good way to say 'hi'," the lizard said, pulling up his glasses.

"Sorry, I was scared. Please stop eating my Brussels sprouts."

"I can't stop, they're so yummy. Go away, you nosy, brown-haired boy," the lizard replied. This made Sam mad. He thought about picking up the lizard and shaking it.

Seeing the look on Sam's face, the lizard continued, "I'm sorry. I'm really hungry. I'm far away from my home in Wisconsin. Let's start over. My name is Professor Scalious."

Sam reached out to shake his tiny green hand when Professor Scalious said, "Sorry, I don't like germs."

"That's okay. My name's Sam. It's nice to meet you."

Professor Scalious started to stretch. Sam asked, "Are you okay?"

"Yeah. I just think it's time for a little yoga."

"You do yoga?" Sam replied. Professor Scalious nodded at Sam and started to stretch into the downward dog pose. Sam thought he looked sort of weird in the arched position.

Professor Scalious had his head and hands down at the ground with his tail pointing up toward the sky. He asked Sam to join him. Sam agreed. Right away he noticed how much it hurt in his stomach and legs. Sam felt shaky and thought he might fall over. But Professor Scalious encouraged him, "You're doing great! We're

dogs now. Ruff, ruff," he barked. Sam laughed awkwardly, almost falling over.

"I've never met a lizard that could talk, let alone one that was funny," Sam said proudly. Professor Scalious smiled an extra big, cheesy smile and went into a new position. He showed Sam the bridge pose. It was another kind of arch, but this time their stomachs were facing the sky. Sam could feel his arms shaking, trying to hold his body up. At first it was uncomfortable, but then he got used to it. The sun began to set and Professor Scalious saw a bright star as they looked up.

"I wonder why that star is so bright," Professor Scalious observed.

"You like stars, too? I think I might know where we can find the answer." Sam went off and brought back his cat.

"Oh, sweet *meteorite*, that fur-ball is huge!" Professor Scalious shouted in alarm.

Sam chuckled, almost losing his grip on the cat, "Don't worry. This is Venus, my cat. She's nice. She won't eat you. In fact, we have a secret spot on my island that's a great place to look at stars.

We should all go there."

"Really? You would take me to your secret spot?" Professor Scalious asked.

"Yeah. I trust you. I think we're going to be great friends."

"Then what are we doing here? Let's hop to it," Professor Scalious eagerly shouted.

"I'm too tired to go now. Why don't we meet there tomorrow?" Sam suggested.

"Okay. Just give me the time and place. I promise to be there five minutes early. Scientist's honor," he said while placing his hand on his heart.

"See you tomorrow, Professor Scalious!"

OFF TO THE ISLAND

JOI BRADLEY, GRADE 4

"Sam!" shouted his mom. "Where are you?"

"I'm outside," said Sam.

"Well, Sam, honey, we're going on a vacation and we can't bring you. I'm sorry," said Sam's mom.

"It's okay," Sam said.

"Bye, honey. It's time for us to go," Sam's mom said.

His dad shouted from outside, "Don't worry, we're only going to be gone for two weeks!" And Sam's parents left for New Orleans. For some reason, they thought it was fine for them to leave, even though they never let Sam go anywhere.

As soon as his parents were out the door, Sam took Venus and went off to the island.

Five minutes after they got there, Sam saw something digging out from under the ground. It made a rushing sound. Sam exclaimed, "Could it be a mole? But moles aren't on islands!" Sam got scared, because he didn't know what it was.

Then Professor Scalious popped out from the ground and said, "Whew, kid! Where's the bathroom? I have to use it, but first I want to see how you made it, because there might be other bugs crawling out from it. If there are flies, I'll catch them with my tongue for lunch. I didn't have any yet anyway!"

Sam said, "Oh no, there's no bugs crawling from it, because ships from Illinois send us bug spray."

When the professor went into the bathroom, he dug in his pocket for a lizard-sized ladder. He climbed up and looked inside the toilet to check for bugs. But when he looked inside, the water rushed out and knocked him off his ladder.

"WhooooOOOOOAAA!" cried Professor Scalious.

The professor came out of the bathroom soaking and angry. But he didn't show Sam he was angry because he didn't want Sam to know—if Sam knew, he might ask questions, like, "What happened?" and then Professor Scalious would feel embarrassed.

Instead, Professor Scalious looked into his pocket and gave Sam a gold watch.

Sam said, "Oh, a watch. What for?"

The professor told Sam, "This watch isn't an ordinary watch! When we fix it up, it's going to be a time-traveling watch! If it works, you can go back in time, and when you want to come back to the present day, you just press the button labeled 'P' for present day."

Sam said, "Wow, this sounds cool! Let's start working."

They went to the old amusement park part of the island and started to work on the watch. As they were working, Sam asked the Professor how he got himself to talk.

The professor told Sam he made a potion and drank it. After a while he started to talk in a human language. Sam asked the professor what potions he used.

"I used garlic, vinegar, sea salt, ketchup, mustard, and...a little bit of pollen and a little bit of snake skin."

In Sam's mind, he thought the professor was a little crazy. Then Sam said, "I like you. Let's be friends now since I got to know you."

Professor Scalious told Sam more about himself, "I don't do much at home, but I like to study in my lab."

Sam told the professor he loved to drink coconuts from the island. The professor thought about it and he asked Sam if he could go get some coconuts from the tree.

"While we're working we can drink coconuts," he said.

While they tried to fix the watch, Sam asked the professor to teach him how to set the watch whenever he wanted to go to a different time. The professor wanted Sam to use the watch to go back in time so they could study dinosaurs. Sam thought this was a great idea, because he loved dinosaurs, too.

When they tried the watch, it still didn't work, so they spent the rest of the day drinking coconuts and working on it. Sam and the professor turned out to be friends, and they got along while they worked together. Sometimes they asked each other what to put here or there. Sam and Professor Scalious were a great team!

PRETTY GOOD FOR TWO FRIENDS

AUDRIANNA WALLER, GRADE 4

The two friends first woke up on the island in front of a lake that looked as big and blue as the ocean. Splashes of water woke them up. Right in front of Sam and Professor Scalious was a hut. By the side of the hut, there was a restaurant sign Sam had made that said COCONUT MILK, hanging on a hollow-made bar.

"Wow, what a sunny day!" Professor Scalious thought. He looked around and saw his new friend Sam. Sam's hair was all poky from sleeping, and he was wearing a dark red shirt and blue jean pants.

"What kind of breakfast is there?" asked Professor Scalious.

"Waffles!" said Sam. "Chocolate waffles."

Professor Scalious felt happy because they were his very favorite kind of breakfast.

After they ate, they walked around the island and found some

clay. They decided to make statues of themselves—they were going to be six feet tall! It took them five hours to build the statues, but when they were finally finished they stepped back and liked what they saw. They looked at each other and both of them said at the same time, "It's pretty good for two friends!"

Later in the day, the new friends drew pictures in the sand with sticks. Professor Scalious drew a picture of himself in his science lab, and Sam drew a picture of himself and his uncle playing tag—even though he liked being on the island, he still missed his uncle sometimes when he was away from his family. They gave comments on each other's pictures.

Professor Scalious told Sam, "Nice drawing of your uncle."

Sam told Scalious, "Nice laboratory!"

The two friends started talking about their lives, and they talked about their favorite hobbies, too. After this conversation, they started to feel happy.

"My teacher calls me Sammy, but you can call me Sam," said Sam.

Professor Scalious responded, "My name is Professor Stephen Scalious but my friends call me Professor Scalious."

Sam showed Professor Scalious around his island. They agreed that their favorite parts were the gigantic pool, the view from an old hotel, and a museum with all sorts of things in it that Sam's great-great-great-great grandfather had built.

"You have a great island," said Professor Scalious.

At the end of the day, Sam took Professor Scalious to the amusement park. They went down a bright yellow slide, and felt like they were on a rollercoaster. The sky was getting dark.

"Will we play again?" asked Professor Scalious.

"Yes, we will play tomorrow!"

After their conversation, they ate dinner. Sam made them both veggie burgers and fries, because they both said it was one of their favorite meals. As they ate, they were happy to be friends.

Finally, they went to bed and looked at the stars, which they both loved. Both of them went to sleep. Professor Scalious dreamed Sam built him a laboratory on the island, and Sam dreamed his uncle was there. Both of them knew this day would be remembered. They both wondered what tomorrow would be like ...

THEY ONLY SPEAK POETRY

JASON BROWN, GRADE 8

In addition to his interest in mapping the tunnel, Professor Scalious had set out in search of the perfect poem. He kept on searching until he came upon Sam. As they became friends, Sam and Professor Scalious talked for a long time about poetry. Sam asked the professor why he loved poetry so much. The professor started his story:

"I used to live under a plastic rock in Wisconsin, in an aquarium. Someone walking past once dropped a sheet of what they were reading."

"What were they reading?" Sam asked.

"I was getting there! They were reading poetry. It was the most beautiful thing I have ever read. Since then I've wanted to write poetry."

"What is so good about poetry?" said Sam.

"It's great! It makes me feel like I am alone on an island with nothing else. Just me, and my poetry, and the calm sound of the ocean."

"I know this place, where they only speak poetry," said Sam.

"Where, where? Tell me!"

"Paris," said Sam, slowly. "It's east of here."

"Really! I want to go there one day," said Scalious. "What do you think it's like in Paris?"

"Well I heard they have a large tower."

"That must be awesome to stand on and look off of...What else?"

"That's the only thing I know of the place."

"Oh. Do you think I would fit in with the people?"

"No!" said Sam.

"Why?"

"You're a lizard!"

"Hey. Do you know why they speak poetry?"

"No, but you should go and ask them. Why did you set out for the perfect poem?"

"I lived under a rock with one poem. I needed more," said Scalious. "I thought that they spoke poetry in other places."

"They do. If you do go to find the perfect poem, I want to go with you," said Sam. "But I don't think my mom would let me."

"Why do you want to go?" asked Professor Scalious.

"What you told me about poetry got me into it. I want to feel like I was on an island with the nice sound of the ocean, too," said Sam. "I want to go to find the perfect poem that has things in it about life and the world."

AN ISLAND OF HIS OWN:
A Poem by Professor
Stephen Scalious, for Sam

DASHYONNIA REDMOND, GRADE 8

Sam is a boy,
a boy that lives on a farm.
Sam snuck his soul away
to the midnight light of the island,
an island of his own.

Sam is a boy,
a street-smart boy,
someone who casts his soul away
by the midnight light of the island,
an island of his own.

The island is a small island
full of colorful trees big and small,
an island full of a beautiful sunset—
its colors of red, pink, orange, purple, and blue
bend in so beautifully it causes his
soul to cast away to the island sunset,
an island of his own.

Sam is a boy,
a street-smart boy,
a boy who no one in school
would think is someone
who casts his soul away to the sunset colors of the island,
an island of his own.

A boy with a cat
named Venus
(a cat I really don't like,
a cat that gets on my nerves, all she does is meow).
They leave and sail away
with the stars and constellations of the island,
an island of his own

Sam is a boy,
a boy that loves his small island.
The island, full of trees of all kinds,
a place where the sunset of its different colors
is beautiful.

He drifts away slow as if he's floating.
His soul casts away to the island,
an island of his own.

A NEW EXPERIMENT

NANCY RUIZ, GRADE 6

Sam was walking around his island with his cat Venus, looking for Professor Scalious.

"Where are you, you sneaky little lizard?" yelled Sam. He was playing hide-a-lizard with Professor Scalious, and Sam had already been looking for an hour. Sam threw some mud at a bush.

"Watch where you're throwing your mud, you mudslinger!" shouted the lizard, doing a backbend.

"What are you doing behind a bush?" Sam asked.

"Doing yoga, what does it look like?" the tiny lizard asked, as he came out of his backbend.

Sam laughed really hard and said, "It's getting late. I think we should be getting ready for bed. I made you a little bed while I was looking for you."

Sam lay on a tree branch, and Venus crouched down to lick her paws. Before he went to bed, Professor Scalious brushed his teeth with a little piece of pinecone he'd found on the ground—he'd attached a leaf stem to it so it looked like a toothbrush. The lizard spit out the sap from the pinecone and accidentally hit Venus in the eye.

Venus hissed loudly in anger. Professor Scalious was so scared he fell back and scurried away. Professor Scalious kept running, even though Venus wasn't chasing him. Eventually, he stopped for a break and fell asleep.

When Professor Scalious woke up, he looked around to see if Venus was watching him. He'd had a dream that he was flying away from Venus. "I wish I had wings, and could fly in real life!" he said out loud.

Venus was not watching him, but Professor Scalious was

still scared, and headed back to find Sam. On the way, he started thinking about what he could use to try and make wings for himself.

All of a sudden, he heard, "Hey, Professor Scalious, where are you? Where did you go last night?"

It was Sam, calling from the top of another tree he had climbed. Professor Scalious yelled back to him, "I'm down here!"

Sam climbed down the tree and Professor Scalious was there waiting for him. "I was hiding from Venus because I was afraid she was going to eat me," said Professor Scalious, "but I have an idea for a new experiment."

"What's your idea?" asked Sam.

"It's wings. I'm going to see if I can make them out of cardboard," said Professor Scalious.

"We need cardboard," Sam exclaimed. "I used to have a ton of it in my house, but we finally got rid of it. I know where to find some more, though. There's a cardboard factory a few miles from my farm! You can go there tomorrow!"

OPHELIA AND SCALIOUS MEET

COBY AKINS, GRADE 6

Ophelia was having a frustrating day. She was working on a new type of cardboard that would be stronger so stuff wouldn't fall through it, but it wasn't working. She was trying to put a protective shield over the cardboard to make it stronger and was using some disgusting-smelling chemicals to do it, but every time she poured the chemicals on the cardboard it would explode.

"Oh my gosh!" she said. "Why does it keep doing this? I know I planned it out correctly!"

Ophelia got really aggravated, so she went outside to calm down and walk around and think about how to make the invention better.

She was walking through the park next to the factory and almost stepped on the strange-looking lizard who was walking toward her in the tall grass. He seemed to be thinking out loud and had his

tiny hand on his chin. Ophelia just kept walking, thinking she was imagining things.

Just then, she stepped on a wire in the grass and there was a small explosion. More explosions! Ophelia couldn't believe it! She was a little scared, and a little curious.

"Pardon me, madam!" said Professor Scalious. "How did you find that wire? I thought I buried it deep into the grass. I'm very sorry I scared you."

Ophelia was shocked, and then she really thought she was imagining things. She saw a rock out of the corner of her eye and picked it up and threw it at the lizard. Quickly, he pulled out a ray gun and zapped it! Lightening shot out the ray gun and the rock turned into ashes.

Ophelia was stunned. Even more so when the lizard said, "Is this how you say hello? Geez! What, you've never seen a talking lizard?"

Ophelia said, "Um, no." She felt weird.

Professor Scalious frowned and said, "Oh, right, I'm a lizard. Well, my name is Professor Stephen Scalious and I am a *highly* skilled scientist." He began dusting off his coat.

"Yeah, I can really see that!' Ophelia said. "Wow, how did you make that ray gun? I thought if you zapped something with a ray gun it would turn into pieces, but you made it turn into little ashes."

"I don't know that much about you yet, so I can't tell you too much information about my science projects. It's possible you are out to steal them."

"Who *are* you?"

"*Hello?* Scientist coat? I'm a mad scientist, of course."

"Well, yeah, I see that, but you...you are a lizard!"

"I may be small, but I have a brain the size of that rock you tried to hit me with!" He stood up as tall as he could and straightened his coat proudly. "Sorry, I really don't have time to chat. I'm on my way to get some cardboard for my newest experiment."

"Hey! I work at the cardboard factory!" Ophelia yelled with surprise. "If you tell me how to work that ray gun, I can get you some cardboard."

Professor Scalious wasn't sure he trusted the girl yet.

"Um, okay. When I press the trigger, two chemicals combine to make a reaction," he said.

This wasn't the truth. He thought he might tell her later, if she seemed okay.

"Okay, cool. I'll sneak you into the factory in my coat pocket."

Professor Scalious entered the cardboard factory and saw lots and lots of cardboard and people making more. It smelled like paper and working machinery. Ophelia snuck him into her office, where she showed Professor Scalious all of the cardboard.

Professor Scalious looked at her strangely.

"What is all this?" he asked.

"This is an invention I've been working on," said Ophelia with a sigh. "I'm trying to make a super-strong cardboard, but it's just not working."

"Wait!" said Professor Scalious. "You're an inventor?!"

"Yes, I am!"

Professor Scalious had a huge smile. This was exactly who he was looking for. Now he could finish his project.

"Well, I can help you!" he said. "Super-strong cardboard is exactly what I need for my experiment!"

Ophelia felt so excited. She couldn't help herself and began blurting out all sorts of science ideas.

"Whoa! Slow down!" said Professor Scalious. "There's lots of time to talk."

"Sorry," said Ophelia, looking a little embarrassed.

"Let's get to those ideas later. For now, we've got some cardboard to make."

Then, Ophelia and Professor Scalious made up a handshake. They knew they were going to be great friends.

THE REUNION

SARA MCDUFFORD, GRADE 3

Professor Scalious said to Ophelia, "You should come back to my friend's island so we can keep working on our super-strong cardboard project."

There was a rowboat by the cardboard factory and Ophelia rowed them to the island. Ophelia saw someone standing on the island waving at them, but all of a sudden she saw a lake-shark and two of his shark friends.

The shark said, "Mmmmmm, that lunch looks yummy to me!"

"I agree with you," said one of his friends.

"Me too," said the other.

Suddenly the sharks were attacked by very hungry leeches who wanted to suck their blood. This gave Ophelia and Professor Scalious time to row past the sharks.

"Whew, thank goodness those leeches got the sharks," said Ophelia.

"I'm with you on that," replied Professor Scalious. "Let's go find my friend."

Ophelia and Professor Scalious had to cut their way through a forest until they got to a pond with beautiful wild animals like deer, snakes, parrots, hawks, butterflies, bugs, frogs, fish, and a squirrel, all getting a drink and resting. They slept by the pond that night.

The next day, Ophelia and Professor Scalious continued traveling and had reached a jungle with a lot of leaves, when they heard talking.

They followed the voices and saw Sam talking to Venus.

Professor Scalious said, "There you are!"

Ophelia screamed with joy. Sam's mouth dropped open. They were really, really excited and filled with lots of joy.

And then Sam said, "Ophelia, is that really you?" He couldn't believe it! Sam thought he would never see his friend again.

"Yes! Is that really you, too?" asked Ophelia.

"Yes! When did you get here?" Sam asked.

"We got here by rowboat yesterday. The professor came to the cardboard factory where I work."

"You work there?" asked Sam.

Professor Scalious said, "Wait, do you guys know each other?"

"We used to be best friends," Sam said.

"It's true!" Ophelia agreed with a big smile.

"Wow, that is wonderful!" Professor Scalious said.

All three had cake and a huge party. Then, they had to row back to the shore before Ophelia was missed at the cardboard factory, but they still celebrated all the way.

Sam and Ophelia were thrilled—they had found each other again! Sam couldn't wait to show Ophelia around his island, but he didn't count on how much work she had to do at the cardboard factory.

SOMEONE HERE TO SEE YOU

CAMERION BLAIR, GRADE 8

"Hey, Ophelia! There's someone here to see you!" yelled Mr. Jenkins (a.k.a. Mr. Aggressive), the cranky old boss in charge of Ophelia's testing station. "You got five minutes!"

But Ophelia knew she only had two. Especially if the boss was having a terrible day.

"Hey, Ophelia," said Sam.

"'Ello, good day, love," said Professor Scalious, acting like a trusty, British sidekick and standing on Sam's right shoulder.

They could tell Ophelia hadn't seen a pillow or bed in ages, seeing that she had on the same clothes from when she had first visited the island a few weeks ago.

"What do you guys want? If you don't mind, I'm trying to create an environmentally-friendly cardboard here!" she piped back at them from behind her workstation, picking away tiny shards of brown cardboard entangled in her frizzy, uncombed hair.

"We want you to break loose from your handcuffs and come to the island with us again," Sam said.

Ophelia let out a deep sigh. "I can't," she said.

"Nonsense!" said the lizard, catching his balance on Sam's shoulder. "This job's got you tied up tighter than a caterpillar inside a cocoon!"

"Time's up, Ophelia," Mr. Jenkins hollered from down the hall.

"Gotta go, bye!" she whispered to her friends before scurrying back onto the factory floor.

Sam just stood there with his mouth wide open.

"Pick up your jaw, dear boy, and let's get going," said Professor Scalious.

The two left the factory and hopped into Sam's canoe outside. Throughout the trip back to the island, Sam kept to himself. The silence was unusual for Sam, who always had something to say about the journey. Every time he got in, he'd either joke to

Scalious about the seat being too hard or how the tiny lizard was rowing too slowly.

But no word came out this time.

"She'll come around in due time," Scalious said from his comfortable seat in Sam's cupped hand.

"I've never been rejected before," Sam said. Then he was quiet for a while.

RINGGGGG!!!!! The alarm clock loudly kicked off the next morning from inside Sam's bedroom on the island. The room was filled with books that he wouldn't dare touch.

"When are you going to get that thing fixed?" Professor Scalious asked groggily as he emerged from the bed Sam had made him out of an old crayon box.

"Soon," Sam replied.

"How soon? I'm tired of hearing that excuse," Scalious grunted. "Wait, where are you going, Sam?"

"For a walk," Sam said, quietly.

Sam stepped outside. He took in a deep breath, filling his nose with the fresh aroma of the lake's ocean-like morning breeze. He loved the way it smelled.

Hearing fish fin-slap the sparkling water and birds chirping, Sam couldn't stop thinking about Ophelia. Every time he thought about her, he'd blush.

After a few days, Ophelia finally agreed to sneak away from work. There is only so much adventure you can have inside a cardboard factory—and besides, she wanted to see Sam and Professor Scalious again.

COME ON THEN!

AYLIN ORTEGA, GRADE 5

Ophelia was up in her office working on a gadget. It was a laser pen she was creating.

"Ophelia!" Her boss was calling. "That boy's here again."

Ophelia ran downstairs. Sam was wearing a white shirt with Brussels sprouts all over it.

"Do you want to come you-know-where?"

"What do you think?" answered Ophelia.

"Come on then!" They both went outside. It was almost dark. Ophelia hoped her parents wouldn't notice she was not coming straight home from work—hopefully they'd just see all the housework being done by her inventions and think she was there somewhere.

The two friends stopped in front of Sam's house, which was old and looked like it was covered in tree bark.

"This way," Sam whispered.

"I know where it is," said Ophelia in a normal voice. Ophelia really wanted to go to the island, because she loved to figure out things on the island. It was the best place for her to concentrate and she wanted to figure out the laser pen.

When they got to the lake, Sam slowly pulled out a small canoe that was hidden behind a bush. Inside it there were paddles and a water gun. They both jumped in. Sam was sitting on one edge of the canoe and Ophelia on the other.

"We better hurry," Sam blurted out.

Ophelia said, "I hope we don't get caught."

Sam reassured her, "Of course we won't get caught—you know a lot."

Sam paddled all the way to a small island. Ophelia continued to work on the laser pen. The wire was disconnected, and the wire she needed was on the island. She thought Professor Scalious could give her some advice, too.

As they paddled, the trees looked mysterious in the dark and it smelled like wet cat and electrical wires burning. When they got there, it was almost midnight. They paddled up to the island and hopped out. They reached back for the canoe and pulled it onto the island near a bush. Under the bush was a secret hideout for the canoe.

Sam's cat Venus came out of the tree and ran to Sam and Ophelia.

A NEW HOUSE

KAITLYN ROMO, GRADE 3

After the laser pen was fixed, Ophelia built a new house out of cardboard for Professor Scalious, Sam, Venus, and herself because she wanted to be nice to her new friends. The house had three cardboards on the bottom, two in the middle, and one on the top. And the top opened up for Sam so he could look at the stars. It had a door that slid open and it was next to a coconut tree.

Ophelia showed them the house when she was finished.

"Oh, why did you do this for us?" said Sam.

Ophelia said, "Because I want us to be close friends."

"What a wonderful person you are," said Professor Scalious.

Professor Scalious had a little nook in the house where he could read his children's atlas, and Venus had a little bed to sleep on. There was even a laboratory where Ophelia and Professor Scalious could work on experiments together.

Later that afternoon, Professor Scalious was reading his atlas, Sam and Ophelia were playing tennis outside next to the coconut tree, and Venus was sleeping in her bed. Venus rolled over when Professor Scalious jumped up (he got excited when he read a cool fact about Europe), and when she rolled over, she hit the wall and knocked the house down.

"Who did this?! Why did they do it?!" said Ophelia.

"Did you jump or something to knock this down?" Sam asked Professor Scalious.

Scalious shook his leg side to side because his head was covered by cardboard. He crawled out from the cardboard and wobbled in circles feeling dizzy.

"Did you do that, Venus?" said Ophelia.

Then Venus looked at Ophelia and nodded, sat down, and made a sad face.

"That's okay. We'll rebuild it!"

They all worked together— except Venus, because she was afraid she would knock it over again. Sam, Ophelia, and

Professor Scalious had fun piling the cardboard on top of each other while they built the house. It only took them fifteen minutes to rebuild it—and it took Ophelia twenty-one minutes when she built the first one. So all three of them dug a pool behind the coconut tree.

"This one looks even better than the other one because we all built it together," said Sam.

Professor Scalious was already playing in the pool.

· ·

Professor Scalious was especially pleased with the new laboratory that they had built out of cardboard. It had been a long time since he'd worked on any experiments and he was looking forward to conducting some new research. Unfortunately, all of his travels had left him a little rusty in the science department, and for a while, he seemed to conduct one bungled experiment after another.

· ·

MONSTER ANT

TAMIA SMITH, GRADE 3

One day, Professor Scalious was working in his laboratory on Sam's island. The professor was watching the inside of a car with his Inside Goggles, which were X-ray goggles he had invented to see how cars work. But then he thought, "This is getting boring, watching how cars work."

He thought of something else to do. He decided to go into his laboratory and start mixing potions. He put on his lab coat. He had desks and computers in the laboratory, and potions on shelves on the walls. He had needles to put the potions inside a potato. The potions were all different colors. He even had one that was black.

Professor Scalious took a red and a pink potion off the wall. "I wonder if mixing these would make a new form of life?" Professor Scalious thought. He was lonely when Sam was at school and Ophelia was at work, and he wanted someone new to talk to. When he mixed the potions together, he gave an evil genius laugh. He wasn't worried about what would happen.

When he mixed some red and pink potions together, a little pink ant appeared. Professor Scalious was shocked. "I didn't mix those potions together for this," he said. He decided to add a little of a green potion, because he was mad that he got an ant, when he could have gotten another professor or something. He thought maybe adding the green potion would turn the ant into a human. So he added the green potion to the mix. Nothing happened at first, and Professor Scalious started laughing, and called the ant a little shorty. The ant got so mad it turned into a big one-eyed monster! The monster was green and gooey, and had one

giant eye that could watch everything. He had two sets of teeth. Professor Scalious was scared of the monster, because he didn't want it to eat him.

"I'm sorry!" Professor Scalious said to the monster. Then the monster turned back into an ant. The ant crawled away and escaped through a crack in the door. Professor Scalious looked everywhere for the ant. He checked all of the windows, but they were all closed. He though maybe the ant was still in the laboratory. But then he got worried that the ant had gotten out, and that if someone stepped on the ant it would get mad and turn into the giant one-eyed green monster again.

A POTION THAT RESEMBLED GREEN TEA

MAXIM ANDRIYCHUK, GRADE 4

Sam's island was not even on the atlas—it was covered in great green plants that hovered over the lake. On this island was the professor's lab. And inside the lab was a potion that resembled

green tea. It was supposed to make the professor bigger and stronger. But instead of taking the potion himself, it accidentally fell into a tank of piranhas, so every five seconds the piranhas grew bigger and stronger.

"Oh dear, oh dear, what will I do? Help! Help!" cried Professor Scalious.

The piranhas didn't like the noise, so they jumped into the ocean. They had grown so big that the tank had broke, and some of the potion fell onto the floor. Professor panicked and began to run away. He didn't know he had the potion on his shoes!

Meanwhile, some of the professor's science friends were visiting him on the island. They were all having a picnic on the island and the potion fell in their drinks! After drinking what they thought was green tea, the potion turned them into giants.

Sam and Ophelia came to visit Professor Scalious then, because they wanted to see one of his experiments he had told them about. They went to his lab first, but he wasn't there. Ophelia saw a bottle with green gooey stuff inside of it and decided to put it in her pocket. Then they heard Professor Scalious call for help, so they followed his voice.

Professor Scalious's four giant-friends felt weird. They thought the professor had made them huge because they had forgotten to invite him to the picnic. So they dug a hole in the path that led to the place where Professor Scalious usually took a break.

When Scalious walked on the hole, the giants pulled him in. Then they had carried him to a table where they tied him up with a cable.

"Make us regular again or we'll make you bald!" all of the giants yelled.

"JINX!" one of the giants shouted. "Knock on wood!"

Whichever giant knocked first would make everyone else owe him a big, generous soda. All four of the giants knocked and each one thought he had knocked first.

"I knocked first!"

"NO! *I* knocked first!"

The giants kept knocking and yelling, and then they accidentally broke the cable tied around Professor Scalious. They stopped arguing and grabbed him before he could run away.

"We'll play dodge ball with you if you try to get out again!" said one giant.

"And you have to buy us all sodas!" said another. "And we'll make you carry them—all of the big, ginormous sodas!"

Sam and Ophelia heard the loud knocking and rushed to find where it was coming from. They finally saw four giants standing around Professor Scalious.

"Hey, giants, what's going on?" said Sam.

"Professor Scalious gave us drinks, but they weren't green tea. They were potions that turned us into giants. And now we want revenge!"

Professor Scalious noticed the bottle sticking out of

Ophelia's pocket.

"Ophelia! You have the antidote to cure my friends! May I have it?" said Professor Scalious.

Ophelia handed the bottle over to Professor and he poured the antidote into the giants' little, normal-person-sized cups. They all chugged it in one sip and they started shaking, and then they turned back to normal.

"Wow..." said the friends, who were not giants anymore. "Thank you."

"Hey, I need to put the antidote in the water, too, so the piranhas will turn back into regular fish and they'll be free!" said Professor. So, he did, and the piranhas were free little fish.

SORRY

JAEDEN WRIGHT, GRADE 3

One day on the island, the professor was working on a science project.

Sam came into the laboratory just as Professor Scalious was finishing a new potion. The professor put the potion in his ray gun—it said "S.R." SHRINK RAY—and as a joke he pointed it at Sam. Sam was shrunk!

When Ophelia heard what happened to Sam, she unshrunk Sam and got mad at the professor. Then Professor Scalious got a lesson. They put him in a pet shop.

He was in a pet shop called *Store for Pets*. The store was filled with dogs, cats, birds, and worse—other lizards! He felt horrible because the animals made loud noises. The birds chirped, the cats purred, the dogs barked, and he hated it! He wanted to escape because it reminded him of his aquarium.

At night, Professor Scalious made an invention called the Laser Ray and he lasered the cage. He raised the window and then escaped. Ten minutes later, Professor Scalious was back in his lab on the island. But all of his rays and his inventions were gone!

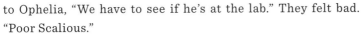

He said, "Sam and Ophelia!" in a mean way. "I should call them."

When he called them he said, "We are not friends anymore."

After the phone call, Sam said to Ophelia, "We have to see if he's at the lab." They felt bad. "Poor Scalious."

Ophelia said, "We owe him an apology."

Sam and Ophelia went to the front door.

Professor Scalious said, "Who is it?"

Sam said, "It's us, Scalious!"

The professor said," Go away!"

Ophelia said, "We're sorry about what we did." Sam and Ophelia had brought back all of his inventions.

"Apology accepted," Professor Scalious said. After that, they didn't argue any more and Professor Scalious was more careful with his experiments.

THE HEROES

BRYAN WILLIAMS, GRADE 4

Sam was riding in his blue car. He built it from branches and leaves. He had a big imagination. He pedaled with his foot. Ophelia had built an airplane out of cardboard. When she was building her airplane, she was thinking about how it was going to feel when she went in the clouds with birds. In the middle of the airplane there was a long, long stick. On the side there were wings, and there was a seatbelt and a control that controlled the wings, and the airplane was pink and white. This was her first time flying an airplane and she was excited. Professor Scalious was wondering about the worms, because why do they come out in the dark instead of daytime? So he decided to use his shrink machine for something useful.

"Ha-ha-ha! All I have to do is shrink and push this button. BOOM! I'm small like a worm," said Professor Scalious in his tiny, noisy voice.

"WOO!" said Sam in his excited voice.

Professor Scalious was underground and Ophelia was in the air.

"I'm in the air!" said Ophelia in her light voice. The plane was working fine but then Ophelia was following a bird and she flapped too hard on the wings and the left wing fell out.

"Aaah!" she said as she fell down. She crashed into the island right by Sam's blue car. Then a worm came back up from its tunnel under the island, followed by Professor Scalious.

Sam said to Ophelia, "Are you okay?"

"Yes, I think so," she said. "Aaaah!" she screamed when she saw Professor Scalious.

"What?" said Sam.

"There's a green worm!"

"No, it's Professor Scalious as a worm," said Sam.

"No, I'm not," said Professor Scalious. "I'm just as small as a worm."

Ophelia got on the ground and Professor Scalious changed back to normal size.

"See?!" he said.

Eating dinner back in their cardboard house, Ophelia said,

"What should we do now?"

"I know!" said Sam. "Let's build an invention."

"But what?" said Professor Scalious.

"I know," said Ophelia. "While I was in the air, I saw bad guys doing crime."

One week passed, and their invention was finished. They all stepped on the machine. It combined the three of them together. They noticed they could scare people with their looks this way. So they flew to the city named Baity City, and landed by a big hotel.

"Everyone stop!" they said.

"You look nasty," the bad guys said.

The heroes—Professor Scalious, Sam, and Ophelia—walked towards them and said, "Stop all of you bad guys. Surrender now."

The bad guys put their hands up and dropped the money and said, "We surrender."

THE BIRTHDAY SURPRISE

EMONI WALKER, GRADE 3

One day, Ophelia was in the island laboratory. Ophelia was building a robot lizard that looked like Professor Scalious as a surprise for him because he had been working so hard at inventing things. Ophelia thought that the robot lizard could make Professor Scalious happy when he was sad. Ophelia made the lizard out of cardboard, glue, chips, cookies, and tape. When the lizard was done it was the same size as Professor Scalious and looked a little like him, but it didn't have a tail as long as Professor Scalious's. Ophelia also made him a little lab coat like Professor Scalious's, only out of paper.

When she was done building the robot lizard, Ophelia went to the island amusement park to meet Professor Scalious. She left the robot lizard in the laboratory so the glue could finish drying. Ophelia met Professor Scalious and they got some ice cream. Professor Scalious got chocolate and Ophelia got vanilla.

Ophelia said to Professor Scalious, "I made a surprise for you. Can you please go to the lab and check on it?"

"Okay," said Professor Scalious. Professor Scalious went back

to the laboratory. When he saw the new lizard, he didn't like it. He saw that the robot lizard looked like him, and he didn't like things looking like him. Professor Scalious went to the front door to go ask Ophelia about the robot lizard. The robot lizard followed him and opened the door, and then closed it just like Professor Scalious did. Professor Scalious was jealous that the robot lizard could do the same things that he could. So Professor Scalious kicked the robot lizard and it broke.

One minute later, Ophelia came back and saw the lizard was broken, and saw that Professor Scalious was tiptoeing away.

Ophelia said, "PROFESSOR STEPHEN! What did you do?"

Professor Scalious said, "I broke it. But I was so jealous of it!"

Ophelia said, "Tell me why you were so jealous of it!"

Professor Scalious said, "Please don't make another robot lizard that can do the same things as me. I was jealous because I want to be the only lizard professor here!"

Ophelia said, "Oh my gosh, you ruined the surprise! It was supposed to be your birthday present for your birthday tomorrow. Professor, you have to help me fix this."

"Are you going to pay me?" Professor Scalious asked.

"No, you're going to have to fix your own birthday surprise."

As Ophelia walked away, she could hear him mumbling about how he didn't want to fix it.

"Professor," Ophelia said, "you FIX it."

So Professor Scalious fixed the robot lizard. Then he threw some confetti up in the air, and shouted "Surprise!" to himself. He started singing "Happy Birthday." Then Ophelia called Professor Scalious and asked him to come into her room. When he got there, the lights came on, and all his friends were there. They yelled, "SURPRISE!"

Ophelia had set the professor up for another birthday surprise, just like the his friends threw him in Germany. She had another robot lizard for the professor. This one was made out of ice cream, which made Professor Scalious very happy.

"That's what I get for breaking the robot," he said.

You're probably thinking that the three friends had seen the last of William Harold James Boogledorf III. They sure thought so. And we wish that was true. But much to the chagrin of Professor Scalious, Sam, and Ophelia, their run-ins with this cantankerous character were far from over.

THE RETURN OF BOOGLEDORF

JENNIFER RESENDIZ, GRADE 5

One sunny Halloween, Professor Scalious was outside getting a tan on the beach near Sam's farm when an old man on a bicycle threw the Sunday newspaper at him.

"HEY! You hit me!" Professor Scalious told the man. "Ouch..." Professor Scalious had turned red.

"Haven't I seen that guy before?" the professor thought.

"I'm so sorry, my name is William Harold James Boogledorf III, but you can call me Boogledorf."

Professor Scalious was shocked. He had heard that incredibly long name before! He remembered everything Boogledorf had done to him in Wisconsin!

"I'm just not going to tell him I remember him," he thought. "If he knows it's me he might freak out again. I'm just going to give him a second chance.

"My, ahh...my...my name is, ahh, it hurts...is Professor Scalious." Scalious was as red as a tomato.

"Oh, well, nice meeting you 'ahh it hurts it is Professor Scalious.' That's a long name."

Boogledorf was a little confused as to how he could meet someone with a longer name than his. He didn't recognize Professor Scalious, because Scalious hadn't had the tan before. Boogledorf hadn't seen a lot of sunburned lizards.

"No, no, no. My name is Professor Scalious."

"Hey, Professor Scalious, I heard they have this awesome film in the movie theatres about peanut butter. Do you want to come watch it with me?"

Professor Scalious didn't really want to be outside anymore

because of his sunburn, so he decided to go to the movie theatre with Boogledorf.

The day passed until both of them were great friends. They went to the store together because they wanted to get some bacon for a snack. Boogledorf was trying to moonwalk because there was a Michael Jackson song on in the store, when he bumped into Ophelia and Sam.

"HEY! Watch it. Never bump into a girl with so many brothers and sisters while she is carrying three bags of groceries!" Ophelia yelled as she turned around and looked very mad. She was about to say, "Hey, you are—!" but Professor Scalious stopped her just in time.

He whispered to her, "Try to pretend you just met him. We're going to give him a second chance."

"Ow, that hu-hu-hurt," said Ophelia to Boogledorf.

"I'm so sorry," said Boogledorf. "My name is William Harold James Boogledorf III." He didn't recognize Ophelia or Sam because he was very forgetful. Unless it was his collection of useless facts or his favorite kind of frostings (strawberry), he was not very good at remembering things. He was happy about meeting new people (even if he had actually met them before).

Boogledorf had a robot voice and every Halloween he dressed up like a hot dog. That day, his costume had ketchup, sprinkles, and frosting on it. Ophelia wondered, "How does a hot dog have a robot voice?"

Professor Scalious was pretending he didn't know Sam and Ophelia so it didn't seem strange to Boogledorf.

"Hello, 'Ow, that hu-hu-hurt.' My name is Professor Scalious.'"

Just then, "Party in the USA" came on in the store. Boogledorf started to break dance with Sam. "Hi, my name is Boogledorf, just Boogledorf."

Everybody got together and started to break dance, and they all decided they would be best friends. Sam and Ophelia started to think, "Boogledorf's actually really fun and cool. Maybe we should just tell him we've seen him before."

But as Boogledorf was break dancing, he started to throw everything in the store. He was throwing food and even Ophelia's grocery bags!

She screamed at Boogledorf and said, "Stop it! You're starting to be annoying."

He just stared at her with a mean look and said slowly, "You know, the average person thinks of bacon 1,000,000 times a second." Then he started break dancing again.

Later that day, Boogledorf had been bumping into everyone.

"Booty-bounce, ha! Sam, you look horrible today, ha ha ha!"

Sam's face was turning so red that he looked like he was going to explode. Boogledorf was messing with everyone. Sam, Scalious, and Ophelia thought of getting revenge on Boogledorf, and they did. "Let's give Boogledorf a little surprise," they said.

Every Sunday, Boogledorf threw newspapers at a super scary house. People said on Halloween the house eats people, even kids, but Boogledorf didn't believe it.

Later that afternoon, Sam hid by the bushes in the house.

"Ah-ha! Take that, house!" Boogledorf yelled as he threw a newspaper. Sam threw the newspaper back at him from his hiding place and Boogledorf jumped in surprise.

"Aaaahh! It's alive, ahh!" Boogledorf was scared and ran away.

"We scared him!" Ophelia yelled. The three of them decided to go to Sam's house to trick-or-treat and also break dance. It was especially nice without Boogledorf there—no one got booty bounced and nothing got thrown.

A VISIT TO
THE MUSEUM

OMAR MIRANDA, GRADE 2

The next day, Sam wanted to go to a museum to see dinosaurs and bones and rocks of the dinosaurs. Sam had never seen dinosaurs up close. He was really excited to see a T. Rex because the T. Rex was a big meat-eater.

Sam, Ophelia, and Professor Scalious used the professor's DriSub® to dig their way there. The DriSub® shoveled the mud out from their tunnel and as they popped up into the museum, they found themselves right next to the T. Rex! Then they found another dinosaur called a Spikosaur that had holes all over its back. It was kept in a big cage-looking thing in an exhibit. They all ran when they saw the Spikosaur and hid behind a wall.

Everybody was scared, but Sam was curious.

Behind the wall, they found a lot of pictures of dinosaurs. They looked at them and discovered what the Spikosaur had on its back—when somebody touched it, spikes popped out of its back and they poked the person like a porcupine.

"That's cool!" said Sam.

"That's NOT cool!" said Ophelia.

"STOP!" Scalious said to Sam.

But Sam went to the cage and tried to touch the Spikosaur, because he didn't believe the spikes would pop out. The others were too afraid to do anything.

A worker at the museum caught Sam just in time, and took

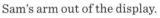

Sam's arm out of the display.

"You could've gotten spiked! That dinosaur is dangerous!" said the worker.

"Thanks," said Sam.

Ophelia and Professor Scalious had cried because they thought Sam was going to get spiked. They were happy he didn't.

They all got hot chocolate in the corner by the waterfall to celebrate how Sam didn't get spiked.

Sam said, "Let's call the Spikosaur *Bob*."

And Ophelia said, "That's a good idea."

. . . .

Sam couldn't stop talking about dinosaurs and how cool the exhibit had been. He decided that he'd use dinosaurs as the topic for his science project back at school, and Ophelia—who loved a good project—volunteered to help him.

. . . .

THE SCIENCE PROJECT DEBACLE

SESASH GUTIERREZ, GRADE 4

"Come on," Sam said when he got back from school and found Ophelia back on the island. "My science project is due next week!"

"I know, but I can't leave Professor Stephen Scalious all alone. Plus, I was in the middle of our project when you came," said Ophelia as she led Sam to the laboratory. She had lots of clear measuring cups and a big and dusty book full of potions all over her cardboard desk. Everywhere there were crazy experiments that she had tried and failed. For this experiment, there were different liquids on one side of her desk and there were cups full of them on the other. In the corners were little plates with different kinds of powders.

"Wow!" said Sam. "I might as well leave. You're nearly done!"

"Oh, no you don't!" said Ophelia when she pulled Sam into the room again. Ophelia was planning to test liquids with different substances to see the reaction. Ophelia usually gave Sam all the small reactions because she couldn't trust him with the big ones. He usually ended up spilling something or breaking it, just like her brothers and sisters.

Next to the experiment, Ophelia put a cup full of pencils. Sam needed a place to put his laser pen, because he wanted to get started on his experiment. He put it in Ophelia's cup of pencils.

There were two liquids. One had water and a lot of baking soda with green food coloring. The other one was the same color but only had vinegar.

"Pour the green liquid with the baking soda," said Ophelia to Sam as she was naming each thing.

"Which green?" said Sam, looking at the two green liquids.

"The green!" said Ophelia, without looking back.

"Okay," said Sam, grabbing a random cup, then—

POOF!

The floor started to shake and the room spun fast.

"What's happening?!" said Ophelia, in a shaky voice.

"I don't know!" Sam responded. Then, it stopped. It was silent for a moment, then Ophelia suggested, "Let's go outside."

"Yeah, I need some fresh air after this shake," said Sam, feeling a bit sick.

Ophelia started walking out and noticed Sam going toward her desk.

"The door is this way, Sam," called Ophelia.

"I know, I just need to get my pen," Sam said.

Then both of them went out the door.

"Wow!" they said, looking at a mysterious wonder. Behind them was a big mountain with caves inside. There were dried up campfires everywhere. Most of all, in the distance, they heard a bunch of drums and could hear cheers from dancing people.

"I bet we're in cavemen time!" said Ophelia. "Cool! But how did it happen?" She thought for a moment and then turned to Sam. "You!" she said.

"It's not my fault! You're the one who didn't tell me which mixture to use!" said Sam angrily.

"Well, if you had listened to me, this wouldn't have happened!" yelled Ophelia.

"But I thought you said this was cool," Sam said.

"Well, yes, but how will we get back? This is all your fault!"

"Well, just because you're so smart does not mean you're always right and, better yet, I bet I can get off this island without you or your help!" Sam yelled, as he walked off.

"Fine. Do it your way!" said Ophelia, going the opposite direction.

Later that day, Ophelia wanted to make a sort of tent to sleep in by the laboratory stairs. She had everything to build it, but didn't know how to do it. On another side of the island, Sam knew how to build a tent, but did not have things to do it. Ophelia and Sam found out that if they were going to get out of this time period, they would need to do whatever it took, but do it together. That night when they were on their way to the tent to sleep, they  heard some unfamiliar voices. It didn't even sound like voices, more like angry sounds.

"What's that?" said Ophelia nervously.

"Don't know," Sam responded.

"Have you put blankets in our tent, Sam?" asked Ophelia.

"Yeah, and did you put other sheets on the top of our tent?" asked Sam.

"Yes," she said.

"So let's go in." And they did. They went in their tent and snuggled in their sheets and slept.

The next day, Sam and Ophelia were awoken by weird talking. Both of them went outside and saw a group of cave people.

"Uh, hello," said Sam in an unfamiliar voice.

The people started talking. Finally one stood and said, "Hello, friends of ours, do you wish to eat?"

"Uh..." said Sam, looking down at a basket of fruits.

"Hello, I'm Ophelia and this is my friend Sam," said Ophelia. "We would be honored to eat with you. Right, Sam?"

"I guess," Sam said, sitting down and grabbing an apple.

After the meal, Ophelia asked the man who had spoke, "Where do you live?"

"Mountain, in caves," he answered.

"Oh," she said.

Later, Sam and Ophelia helped search for food.

"Sam and Ophelia, you will help cook," said the man.

"All right," they said. They went with a lady and copied what she did. Sam and Ophelia saw her take a sharp stone and wipe it with a wet leaf. Ophelia followed while Sam used his laser pen to cut. The heat from the laser cut the fruits and veggies and some meat. Back at the group, they all sat and ate lunch: vegetables in water with mushed tomato.

"Yum. Simple but great," said Ophelia. "Don't you think, Sam?"

"Oh, um, not bad," he said with vegetable pieces and tomato around his mouth. "It's better than Brussels sprouts."

"Right," said Ophelia with a small laugh.

Sam wiped his face with a leaf. It was silent for a moment, and then Sam said, "Sir, why do you speak English while the others do not?"

The man gave a sigh and answered. "It was ten years ago when I was an inventor. I made a time machine to show how things change over time. When I came to this time period, my machine broke and disappeared. Now, I am stuck here, and the time has turned me into one who would have lived here. Soon this will happen to you if you stay."

"No!" said Sam, imagining himself as a caveman. "Ophelia, we need to get out!"

"Okay, so how did we get here?" she asked.

"Well," said Sam. "I got a clammy-looking green liquid and kind of spilled it on the machine, and the container switched something."

"Clammy, green liquid," whispered Ophelia herself. "Ah-ha! You got the vinegar and it must have poured on the front microchip and then the switch must have activated it!"

"Yes, but is the time machine still here?" wondered Sam.

"Let's go see in the lab," said Ophelia. "Sam, Sir, let's go." The three of them went in the lab and saw it.

"It's still here!" Ophelia said with excitement.

"But the liquids aren't," admitted Sam, looking at them on the floor.

"I know a potion that is very similar to vinegar, water, and baking soda," said the man.

"Thank you—" said Sam, but stopped. "That reminds me...what is your name, anyway?"

"Lee," he said.

"All right, Lee, tell us where to go," said Ophelia. Lee led them to a river next to bushes and trees.

"Sam, get me a bowl with water," he said, handing him a bowl. "Ophelia, get me ten olives off of that tree," he said, pointing to the tree.

Ophelia dipped the bowl in the river and got water, and Sam climbed the tree and put ten olives in her free hand. Lee got a stick and put some fuzzy-looking berries in a small grey bowl made of stone.

"Why can't you get it with your hands?" asked Sam.

"They itch," Lee responded. Then all of them headed back to the lab, and, there, Lee mixed the water with the olives and put pieces of the fuzzy things and berries onto a plate.

"Now, about the heavy thing being pushed, it had to be a lever," suggested Lee.

"The problem is, it's not here!" mentioned Ophelia.

"Hmmm, we need something ... not long, but that can send a sort of signal to activate this thing," said Lee.

Sam was playing with his laser when Ophelia yelled, "Like that!" She pointed at the laser pen.

"Great! Not long, but thin!" said Lee.

Sam was chosen to put it where the lever used to be, and turned the laser on. He was about to let out his ray of light when he saw Lee going.

"Lee, come on," Sam told him.

"No, I belong in the past. You go," Lee told them.

"Don't you want to come?" Ophelia asked.

"No, I need to stay for the next people who come," he admitted.

"All right," they both said. "Goodbye, Lee!"

Sam turned on his laser. The room spun, the ground shook, Lee disappeared, and then it stopped.

Everything was normal when Ophelia and Sam came out: the trees and the big hill, the small pond, and their lab. Most of all, no time passed.

"Hey, we still need to do my project!" Sam whined.

"Okay, I have an idea. Let's just do a baking soda volcano with red food coloring in the soda and vinegar!" said Ophelia.

"Right," said Sam. "But I will be more careful."

"You got that right," joked Ophelia.

While Sam and Ophelia were working on Sam's science project— and doing some unintentional time-travelling—Professor Scalious was having a few problems of his own. Actually, it was mainly one problem—a small, orange, Siamese problem named Venus.

IN VENUS'S STOMACH

ISMAEL IRIZARRY, GRADE 3

Venus and Professor Scalious were working on a new teleporting invention. They made it for hide-and-seek and also to go anywhere at once. It was made out of titanium and was as big as an elephant. There were two sides to it: one for Venus and one for Professor Scalious.

Venus pushed one of the buttons and Professor Scalious ended up in Venus's stomach. (This button was secretly installed by Venus herself. It had a picture of Professor Scalious's face on it.)

Once inside Venus's stomach, which was full of fish bones, Scalious screamed, "Get me out of here!!!" A fish bone poked at Professor Scalious's scales.

Sam was calling for Professor Scalious then, because no one knew he was in the cat's stomach. Professor Scalious started running in circles so Venus would get dizzy and throw up and he could get out. It worked!

"Venus, why did you press the button? You crazy cat!" said the professor.

"I just wanted to have some lunch!" Venus replied with a meow.

Professor Scalious knew he could no longer trust Venus, so he teleported her into a big tank of water with a remote control shark. He teleported her back after a few minutes and Venus shook her paws in the air and meowed, "I will plot my revenge!"

After that, Professor Scalious made more inventions and Venus ate more fish bones.

WHY CATS MAKE TERRIBLE PETS:
An Essay by Professor Stephen Scalious Written for Sam's Consideration

PENELOPE SYMONDS, GRADE 7

My name is professor Stephen Scalious. I have studied cats during the early years of my life and have come to the conclusion that cats make terrible pets. Unlike calm, patient lizards — like myself — cats are crazy and hyper. Cats are terrible creatures. They do not make good pets. Cats are bullies — they are not friendly, and they destroy habitats with their gigantic claws.

One time, I was minding my own business when an evil cat with big fangs jumped in front of me and knocked me off my feet with his big paws. Another time, I was walking around the Wisconsin Blue Aquarium and a giant, fat cat grabbed my tail with its paws. He was about to eat me when my best friend came to my rescue. Unlike cats, reptiles such as myself and my friends are helpful to others. We never pick on animals smaller than ourselves. Cats are rude and they have no right to be picking on someone smaller than

162

them. Cats should pick on someone their own size.

Cats make terrible pets because they are not friendly. One time, I was in the aquarium and I saw a person eating a cracker while petting a cute little kitten. All of a sudden, the kitten clawed and hissed at the human! In all my years of studying animal behavior, I have learned that no other animal hisses or claws like cats do. When was the last time you saw a goldfish jump up and hiss at you? When was the last time a snake slithered up to you and clawed at you? Kittens may look cute and innocent, but they are not.

Cats make terrible pets because they destroy habitats for other animals. Once, I made an awesome couch for my plastic rock using sticks. While I was trying to get the couch into my cage, a cat jumped out at me and then knocked my couch to the ground, destroying it into hundreds of tiny pieces. They also destroy other animals' habitats and sometimes harm them. I have observed that cats  destroy fish tanks to get to the fish inside. I have also observed cats trying to knock down birdcages.

I suggest that you, Sam, should research your options on different pets. I have done research on pet behavior and have seen that about 95% of cat owners think that cats are crazy and hyper. On the other hand, 95% of birds, reptiles, and fish are calm and friendly. If you want a relaxed life, I suggest you do not keep Venus for a pet. I recommend that you get a bird, reptile, or fish as a pet because they are not bullies. They are friendly, and they do not destroy furniture.

Sam didn't go for the essay. He tried to explain to Professor Scalious that Venus was really a very sweet cat who would surely never try to eat a lizard. The professor was probably just imagining things. Besides, Sam couldn't just get rid of her—Venus was his friend. Professor Scalious sighed, realizing that there was no reasoning with Sam. He was blinded by love. Professor Scalious would have to take matters into his own hands.

THE NICEANATOR

GRACE WHITESIDE, GRADE 3

One day, Professor Scalious was in the laboratory in his cardboard house, surrounded by potions, jars of brains, and books of poetry. Venus was still trying to eat him when Professor

Scalious shoved Venus into his "Niceanator," which was made out of turkey sandwiches. In a minute Venus jumped out of the Niceanator and scurried over to Professor Scalious and hugged him so hard he couldn't breathe! Professor Scalious was happy he made Venus nice, but also didn't want Venus hugging him everyday! But he had already made his choice, and couldn't change it. And after that, Venus didn't try to eat Professor Scalious anymore.

The next morning, Venus woke up Professor Scalious with a tight hug. Professor Scalious was FURIOUS! He didn't want Venus waking him up every day at 6:00 a.m. After a while, Professor

Scalious went back to sleep.

The next day, Ophelia came to see Professor Scalious. They talked about a new invention called the "Ratanator." With it Venus wouldn't hug Professor Scalious, because she would be busy chasing thousands of rats instead.

"We are geniuses," said Professor Scalious, giving Ophelia a high-five.

They were so happy, they were running around the house. Then Sam came in, and he accidentally tripped on the Ratanator and then had rats all over him!

"Oh my gosh!" said Sam.

They got the rats off of Sam by using a magnet, because all of the rats were made out of metal.

Deep down, Professor Scalious actually liked Venus—when she wasn't trying to eat him—and he knew how special Venus was to Sam. He decided he'd try to resolve their problems once and for all by inventing a new concoction to help them communicate better.

TRYING TO TELL YOU

MAJA RIVERA, GRADE 3

In Professor Scalious's lab, the professor was working on an experiment to know what Venus says when she meows. He decided to make a potion so he could help Venus if she had any problems and if she needed something. Professor Scalious was also a little scared of Venus, since Venus was much bigger than he was.

"MEOW!" Venus screamed sadly. She was kind of uncomfortable.

Professor Scalious thought Venus's face looked hungry and scared.

"She might want to eat me!" thought Professor Scalious. He was shaking with fear.

Venus jumped toward him. Professor Scalious thought, "Oh no! She *really* might want to eat me. I bet I look tasty!" Professor Scalious was also thinking, "How can I understand Venus?"

He decided to make a potion out of palm tree bark (so it wouldn't taste disgusting), some human DNA, and a lot of juicy island fruit like pears, tangerines, and strawberries.

Because it smelled great, Venus tried the potion. She started meowing weirdly.

"Mrrow. MEE-OW! MEE-OW! Mrrow-eat. Mrrow-food." She sounded really sore because her stomach was hurting.

Professor Scalious was surprised.

"Are you all right?" he asked.

Suddenly, the meowing stopped.

"My stomach's hurting," said Venus. "Can you help me?"

Her voice sounded like a kid voice.

"Wow!" Professor Scalious said. He jumped up and down, sort

of crying inside. Since he was a scientist, he thought he might have some medicine to help her stomachache. Scalious looked in his cabinets and found a bottle full of medicine to make the pain go away. It was in a little blue bottle. He mixed it with yummy cat food to make it taste better.

Venus tried it.

"I feel so much better and freer now," said Venus. "Thanks a lot! I've been trying to tell you that my stomach was hurting and I needed your help for a really long time!"

After that, they became really close friends and Professor Scalious would always scratch behind Venus's ears because cats really like that.

ONE MORE CHEMICAL

MARTEZ CROSBY, GRADE 8

"I'll just need one more chemical," said Professor Stephen Scalious. He put the batteries into the machine and then *BOOM!* The machine exploded. The professor was crying. Ophelia burst into the lab. "Professor, what happened?" she said.

"Nothing. I'm just a failure," said the Professor.

"No you're not," said Ophelia. "You invented cures for diseases. You made cars that can fly. You made flying *shoes*, for crying out loud. You can do anything."

"Oh fine, I'll do it. What chemicals do I need?" said Professor Scalious.

Ophelia said, "I might have a solution. Let me work on the invention!"

The professor said, "No, thanks. I know I can do it alone."

"Okay, good luck," Ophelia said and left.

Ten minutes later, the professor yelled, "I'm done."

Ophelia burst into the room. "You're done! Let me see…What is this? This isn't the machine," she said sarcastically. "This is a poem called 'The Professor Who Couldn't Make a Simple Machine.'

I can make a poem, too:

Roses are Red,
Violets are Blue.
Professor—quit writing poems
and work on the machine, too!"

"Nice Poem," said the professor. "Do you mind if I use that?"

"No," said Ophelia. "But I do mind you writing poems instead of inventing. Otherwise I'm going to work on the machine by myself. Now come on!"

"Fine," said the Professor. "I won't give up."

Ophelia studied the invention.

"Okay. Let's try some ideas," said Ophelia. "Are there any ideas you have Professor?"

"No," he said.

"I've got it," said Ophelia. "Milk! It goes with a lot of science projects."

"Okay," said the Professor. "You work with that while I go get some Brussels sprouts. I'm hungry."

Ophelia poured the milk into the tube. Then the professor came in and tripped over the cord, and the Brussels sprouts went into the tube. The machine rattled, *clinky-clink*, and then suddenly stopped again. After a while, Ophelia found the problem.

"What's wrong with it?" asked the professor.

"We need Brussels sprouts," said Ophelia.

So Ophelia called Sam, who was helping out on the farm that day.

"Hello," Sam answered.

"Hey. I need Brussels sprouts at the lab right now," said Ophelia, and hung up.

NO RAIN:
As Told by Sam

DONTE WILLIAMS, GRADE 8

It had been a week and no rain. For a week the Brussels sprouts hadn't been growing at all. We were not making money and soon would have no food. I was starting to think that we would never have Brussels sprouts again and we'd have to sell the farm to get money.

I went for a walk through the fields and got dazed from the hot sun pouring down on me. I started hallucinating that I was seeing talking Brussels sprouts. They said "EAT ME!" They were like zombies. They were so tall that they were two times my height. I started to get hungry. I ran after one and ended up tripping into the sand. Some sand hit my eyes. It burned. I quickly got out of shock and dizziness.

I got back home, found my canoe, and went to my secret island. Even on the island, the flowers were dying. I was upset about us not having enough money on the farm but then I thought about the bright side—I didn't have to eat those Brussels sprouts every morning.

I ate some candy and sat there thinking about how no rain had fallen. Suddenly, I got a call from Ophelia on the other side of the island. She was really smart, and she always used to get A's in school. That's why they made her take the high school tests.

We talked on the phone to catch up, and she told me why she needed some Brussels sprouts. I told her I'd come as soon as I could. When I got to the other side of the island and found my friends, Ophelia looked wonderful. We went to her laboratory, which was huge! She had all kinds of technology and chemicals lying everywhere. We sat on the couch and thought about what we could do about the rain. We both needed the Brussels sprouts to grow again.

"What do you think we can do?" I asked her.

She replied, "Water comes from the clouds, so I think we should make our own clouds somehow."

We went to find Professor Scalious and asked him how we could make the clouds.

"I have a water chemical," he said, "but all I need is a little bit of smoke."

We grabbed two sticks but they didn't work so we grabbed two stones and kept rubbing them together until a flame appeared. We quickly grabbed some grass and sprinkled it on the rocks. Soon it became a smoking fire.

We tested the smoke with the water chemical and made lots of clouds. Ophelia and I put the clouds in a jet plane with a low temperature so the clouds would not vanish. But just as we were about to release the clouds the jet ran out of fuel and we had to use the clouds as parachutes to get us back to the farm.

We made it back safely with the clouds. We then put the water chemical in the clouds and let them float into the air. Nothing happened. We both thought we had failed the project.

"It didn't work," I said, feeling depressed.

"We did all this for nothing," Ophelia said dejectedly as she fell to the ground with a sad face. "I'll go back to the lab and tell the professor about the failure."

Ophelia had to get home, and I went back to my house and took a rest because I was exhausted.

The next morning, I woke up and did the usual. I walked outside and all I heard was squish and splat! It had rained overnight! I quickly called Ophelia and told her the good news. Then I told my mother and father that we would be making money.

The next week, the Brussels sprouts were ready to harvest. Ophelia came to collect some. She was happy it had rained so she could finish her latest experiment. I thought that even though I didn't like Brussels sprouts, I was sure happy the ugly things were growing at our home again.

....

After the drought, Sam worked extra hard on the farm to help his family. He just needed business to get back to normal, he figured, and then he could finally get back to his adventures.

....

THE BEST BRUSSELS SPROUTS ON THE BLOCK

LUCY NASH, GRADE 3

Ophelia was excited. She knew that today Sam was opening a Brussels sprouts stand to help his parents' business.

"Man, this is as hard as passing an eighth grade test if you ask me!" said Sam, who was only in fifth grade.

The next day, Professor Stephen Scalious was studying a squirrel. "These things are neat!" he said. Then he heard crying. He followed the sound and discovered it was Sam.

"What's the matter?" Professor Scalious asked.

Sam said his Brussels sprouts stand was out of business. Professor Scalious called Ophelia to come over. Next, they all helped solve the problem with Ophelia's new invention, the Taste

2000, which made things taste very good. How it worked was pretty simple: First, it washed the Brussels sprouts and then made the tiniest hole, that even if you used a magnifying glass, you couldn't see. It put in some seasonings such as salt and pepper.

"Wow, how'd you do that?" Sam asked.

"It's easy," said Ophelia.

Professor Scalious asked how Ophelia made the hole so tiny.

"Simple," said Ophelia. "A needle."

Sam and Professor Scalious ate a Brussels sprout. "These taste as good as a Thanksgiving feast!" said Sam.

"It's impossible to fit so much flavor into one Brussels sprout!" exclaimed Professor Scalious. "What a remarkable invention!"

Sam now had the best Brussels sprouts on the block. He could finally go on another adventure!

PART 4

THE LUMPY UNDERWORLD OF IMAGINATION

THE MYSTERY OF THE CHOCOLATE ISLAND:
As Told by Ophelia

ROCKIA TAYLOR, GRADE 8

One day, Sam came to find me at Ten Buck Two, the cardboard factory where I work. He was wondering what type of cardboard box he should use for his next science project.

"Well," I said, "you should get a long, hard cardboard box. Speaking of that, it's time for me to get off of work. Let's go find the professor."

Professor Scalious had gathered up some of his lizard friends for yoga. When the professor was done with yoga, we planned to meet up at our cardboard house to decide where we were going for our big adventure.

The professor said, "One of my friends that I was doing yoga with told me about this faraway island made out of chocolate."

"Wow, that sounds like a great idea. You guys know that I love chocolate!" Sam yelled excitedly.

I said, "Ok, we will go today and take your canoe."

When we got to the canoe, I put the cardboard box in there. Sam said, "Ophelia, go back to the house and get sleeping bags, a first-aid kit, and our food supply. Even though we're going to Chocolate Island, we'll still need milk and water." I returned and we left.

It took us hours to get to Chocolate Island. On the way there, we saw chocolate birds flying around. As we moved along, we saw people in the chocolate lake, playing with one another. I reached down and touched the chocolate water. It felt so soft as I came up with it, and it was going through my hands and back into the lake. I lifted my hands to my mouth to taste it. As it was entering my mouth it tasted like hot chocolate.

We moved deeper into the chocolate land and saw chocolate trees moving around I saw a family of deer run past. As they were galloping, I noticed they kicked up chocolate, because it was hard running through the chocolate grass. I also saw chocolate birds. The mother bird was feeding her baby birds chocolate worms. I was amazed seeing other animals with different skin all made out of chocolate.

As we were looking around the island, we saw a wise, old woman. Sam walked over to the wise woman and said, "Is this a dangerous place?"

The wise woman responded, "This is a great place."

Professor Scalious said, "Look at this place! It is so beautiful. How did this chocolate get here?"

The wise woman said, "It was years ago, people used to travel from all over the world to dump the chocolate that they didn't eat onto the island."

I asked, "How were the trees, grass, and animals made out of chocolate, too?"

She answered, "We're not sure, actually. One day, everything was just here. It's magic. It came from nowhere. I think it's a sacred place. It is my own little island. Few people know about it."

We decided to build a tree house on Chocolate Island just in case we came back and wanted to have shelter. I said, "Okay, Sam and Professor, we should get started on gathering things for our tree house because it is getting dark out."

Sam said, "The cardboard that I got from the factory! We could use it for the tree house, just like on our island."

I saw sticks in the grass and said, "Hey, you guys, we can use these chocolate sticks for our house."

Professor went over to a pile of rocks and brought it back to us and said, "We can use this for our tree house, too!" All of us started bringing more things for the tree house.

Everything went all right as we built the house. Afterward, we needed to put chocolate on top of the house to glue it all together. By the time we were done building our tree house, it was dark outside. We gathered our things, put them in the tree house, and went to sleep.

While we were sleeping, we heard something outside like a wolf howl. It woke us up. We were scared.

I said, "I'll go and check it out." Outside, I saw a gray-brownish baby wolf. It was cute. I decided to go touch it, but as I walked toward it, it ran away.

In the morning as we woke up, we heard sounds coming in our tree house. We walked outside, and found that when the sun came out, it melted the house. We were sad that we had put our hard work into building the tree house and it had melted.

The professor said, "We should get going, because Ophelia has to go to work, I have to do yoga, and Sam has to go to school."

In between his exploits and experiments, Professor Scalious was still a devoted fan of yoga. One day, he came home from a visit to his local yoga studio feeling so good he was inspired to write a poem.

YOGA STUDENT:
A Poem by Professor
Stephen Scalious

KIMBERLY MARTINEZ, GRADE 5

I am a yoga student.
I see people stretching
and listening to music.
It's relaxing too because of the baby-blue-sky wall.
The mat is squishy and I am mad
because the sweat made me fall.
I put the gum in my mouth and was surprised
it was minty. The sweet vanilla-scented candle
makes me hungry just like a bear.
It's quiet with a hum just like bees.

HALF-PARTS LAND

JUSTIN JEFFERSON, GRADE 3

One night, while the three friends were playing on the island, they closed their eyes and Sam imagined a pretend world. When they opened their eyes, Sam's imagination had come true! Sam's world was colorful and had deserts everywhere.

A rock was moving so Ophelia turned the rock over. Then Boogledorf appeared out of a hole, snatched everyone up. He dropped them into the hole that led them to a country called Half-Parts Land.

They called it Half-Parts Land because everything and everyone was two things, like a snake was half-snake and half-bear. Sam turned into a half-boy and half-tiger. Ophelia was half-girl and half-cat. Professor Stephen Scalious was half-lizard and half-owl.

Sam, Ophelia, and Professor Stephen Scalious screamed, "Aaahh! We have to get out of here!"

Then a chocolate bar came by, which was also half-bear. In a deep voice it said, "My name is Macho. The only way you can get out of here is to follow the blue trail." He pointed to a long-winding, bright blue path. It was 500,307,000 miles.

"Let's go!" said Sam.

When they were walking they saw a go-kart. Ophelia said, "Hey, let's jump in that!"

The gang squeezed in and pressed the turbo button. *Vvvvrrrooommm.* The go-kart was going 500 miles per hour! Along the road, they bumped into a huge monster. The monster had 1,000 teeth inside a seven-foot-long drooling mouth. He wore red, blue,

and green-colored clown shoes. He had a bright red nose. His hair was multi-colored and was so big it hovered over them. No light could get through this monster's monstrous hair.

The monster grunted, "I am so hungry!"

The gang was terrified. So they closed their eyes. When they opened them, they found they were inside of the monster's throat. They had been eaten!

Professor Scalious said, "I should use my lizard tongue to tickle our way out of here."

He tickled the inside of the monster's throat until the monster threw them up and projected them into the air so far that they landed only a mile away from home.

They heard a large *BURP*, a burp so loud it shifted the trees and created a wind that swooped the gang right in front of the sign that directed them back home. But the sign was ripped, so they couldn't read where it said how to get back into the hole that would take them home. As they were looking for pieces of the sign, Ophelia fell into quicksand. She grabbed Professor Scalious's hand, who grabbed Sam's hand, and all three of them went underground. They traveled through the lumpy underworld of Sam's imagination and ended up back home on the island, above ground and in reality.

"Phew." Ophelia was relieved.

"Wow!" Sam was excited.

"Oh, no!" Professor Scalious was still a little scared.

Sam and Ophelia never tired of hearing about Professor Scalious's travels around the world. Their favorite story was about Professor Scalious's trip to L.A. because it sounded really cool. One day, Sam said, "Well, why don't we all go there?" No sooner had he suggested it than they were off to the DriSub®.

RETURN TO L.A.

ZOLA A. PRICE, GRADE 6

Sam, Ophelia, and Professor Scalious prepared themselves to be shot out of the ground from deep inside their tunnel. *KAPOW*!

They got up and looked around, and then stared at a big building. It was the Hollywood Wax Museum. Ophelia sighed heavily. Several people stared at them and the strange sight, then continued with their day. Sam was staring in awe at all the tall buildings, which Scalious was rather intimidated by.

The group looked rather out of place in their faded jeans and patched up t-shirts. (Except for Scalious, of course. All he wore was his lab coat.)

"Is there some sort of admission fee?" Ophelia whispered to Sam.

"No one should mind," Sam answered.

Ophelia walked up to the *Wizard of Oz* scene.

"This is cool!" she said out loud.

They wandered into the horror movie part. Ophelia closed her eyes and bumped into something. She whipped around and saw a wax guy with a chainsaw and hockey mask. She screamed and ran into a different room.

"I'm going to check out the horror section for a while longer!" Sam called.

Looking closely at the wax figure of Marilyn Monroe, Ophelia noticed something wiggling in her white dress. She saw a flash of green and all of the sudden Professor Scalious was sitting on her head.

"Thank goodness! I didn't think wax people moved!" Ophelia thought to herself.

Then Professor Scalious jumped onto her foot and grinned.

"Ah, Scalious. Sam and I were wondering where you went."

Professor Scalious was using a computerized translator that day. The translator's computerized voice answered, "Taking notes."

"I wouldn't want to lose you."

Scalious jumped off Ophelia's foot and called, "Taking more notes. See you soon!"

Just then, Ophelia saw an old man carrying a large bag. He had his back to her with his eyes fixated on the wax Teenage Mutant Ninja Turtles. When Ophelia got closer to the man she realized he was staring at a portable television he'd set in front of the exhibit. Ophelia realized something else: it was *her* portable television! It even had her signature on the back! She called out to Sam—however, it was Venus that came to her.

Venus meowed loudly.

"Go find Sam! The DriSub® must have been robbed!" Ophelia said to the cat.

The old man turned to look at her and smiled. Most of his teeth were missing and his hair was a mess. Ophelia recognized him right away. Boogledorf!

Ophelia grimaced with disgust and began to walk backward. She was red in the face with anger and might have swiped her portable television if Boogledorf had not thrown a vanilla cake at her face. Unfortunately, it hit its desired mark.

"Yuck! Vanilla is my least favorite flavor of cake!" she yelled.

"I'm going broke from buying cakes, you know. They used to be a lot cheaper! But my get-rich-quick scheme will take care of that! AHAHAHAHAHA!!!" The old man laughed with glee. "Kermit the Frog is left-handed!" he cried, and with that, flew away.

"Let's get out of here before some other creepy old man hits us with cake!" Sam shouted to Ophelia, and with that he scooped up Venus and began to exit the building. Ophelia stopped him.

"Where is Professor Scalious?! I can't find him anywhere!"

"Let's just get back to the DriSub®!" Sam interjected.

"But Scalious!..." She just wished she knew where Scalious was. A horrible thought crossed her mind. *What if the old man stole him!* She pushed the thought out of her mind and followed Sam into the DriSub®.

"I know we'll find him," she thought. "We have to." Little did she know that the creepy old man could follow them anywhere. His special heat-seeking cake frosting had stuck to her shoe.

Professor Scalious was waiting in the DriSub®.

"I was completely scared to *DEATH*!" Ophelia shouted at him. "Where were you?"

He answered, "Repairing the DriSub® and writing haikus."

"Don't disappear like that again," Ophelia scolded as she climbed into her seat, ready to go home.

On their way back to the island, Sam, Ophelia, and Professor Scalious decided to take in some peace and quiet in the forests of Michigan. But no sooner had they started to relax than they realized something was amiss.

SOMEONE STOLE MY CAT!

SAUL GARCIA, GRADE 4

"Aahh," said Professor Scalious, as he sipped his cocoa.

"This cocoa tastes good," Sam said.

Sam and Ophelia were sitting together on a mini flower-patterned couch and Professor Scalious was across the room, holding his tiny cocoa mug with his tail.

"Can this tree house break?" Professor Scalious asked.

"Nope," Ophelia answered.

This tree house belonged to Ophelia. She had built it with her brothers and sisters in a forest in Michigan, which was the first place she'd been away from home. She liked all the squirrels and birds that lived there. The tallest tree in the forest was where she put her tree house. It was big and green, to go with the trees around it.

"Wh-what?!" Sam yelled out suddenly.

"What's wrong?" Professor Scalious and Ophelia said.

"Someone stole my cat!" Sam screamed.

Both Professor Scalious and Ophelia dropped their cocoa and looked shocked.

"There's a footprint!" Professor Scalious said, pointing at the ground through the hole of the escape pole in the floor.

"My calculations say the thief is far from the tree house, somewhere else," Ophelia said. "He's in the forest..."

"What are we waiting for?!" Sam yelled.

The three of them went down the emergency escape pole and landed on the soft grass. They saw more footprints going into the forest.

"Those footprints look like Boogledorf's feet!" Ophelia said.

"Let's follow the prints!" Sam said.

Professor Scalious got onto Sam's shoulder and they all followed the footprints in the mud. The trail of footprints went on for eight miles, then stopped at a river.

"I'm tired," Sam and Ophelia said.

"Keep moving," said Professor Scalious from Sam's shoulder.

Sam and Ophelia were out of breath from running so far. Then out of nowhere, Ophelia was startled.

"Ahh!" she screamed.

Venus came out of the woods and was so happy that she jumped at Sam and Ophelia.

"OH! Where did you go?!" said Sam.

Venus sniffed the footprints.

"She must have followed these footprints, too!" Ophelia said.

"Did Boogledorf kidnap you?" Sam asked.

Professor Scalious was looking the other way across the river and thought he saw a big shadow far away in the woods.

"Look!" he shouted, waving his arms over at the river.

Sam and Ophelia turned and saw the big shadow, too!

"But maybe it's just a tree shadow..." said Ophelia.

Then the shadow started moving. Was it their imagination or did the shadow have very, very messy hair?!

"LOOK!" Sam said.

But the shadow had already disappeared.

So the three friends went back to the tree house with Venus and enjoyed more cocoa.

Finally, the adventurers made it home.

NO SUCH THING AS A SLIPPERY ROCK

JAVIER PACHECO, GRADE 4

One day, Sam and Professor Scalious were walking and they found Venus was gone again! Sam thought Venus might have been abducted by aliens who thought Venus was *from* Venus. Scalious had positive feelings that there were no aliens. That was when Sam and the professor got separated.

Professor Scalious made special bugs to make him grow bigger and act differently. He made them with oil, some poison, and an antidote to cure his scale virus. By accident, he put in his own DNA. This combination made him huge—alligator-like! Because the professor was a reptile, he had the weirdest look. He had big, large teeth, and big, old eyes, with a green, ferocious face.

Professor Scalious tried to push Sam's canoe so he could get to the other side of the island to find the lost Venus. He made tracks on the way to the canoe with his claws to help Sam find him.

Sam did find the tracks and followed them to the canoe. He thought he heard something. Was someone on the boat? He looked and looked and did not find anybody, but then he saw something move in the water. Sam jumped into the water and when he turned around he saw the alligator-like Scalious. The professor accidentally gave Sam a fierce look.

Professor Scalious was swimming next to two tunnels that were half-filled with water. He dove into one, and Sam, who was a bit frightened, raced into the other.

"Ow!" Sam said. He slipped on what seemed like slippery rocks and then he was swimming. Sam kind of knew that there was no such thing as a slippery rock, so he looked back at it. The light was shining and he saw that it was actually a crystal. Inside the crystal, there was a dinosaur bone. It was made of special glass and ice and there was a T. Rex in it! Since Sam was an adventurer, he was always looking for treasures. But then he remembered that the only treasure he really wanted was Venus.

Sam tried to act like a rat and squeaked, hoping Venus would pounce on him and he could trap her. He tried crawling through on his hands and knees because he thought he could track Venus by her perfume. But when he listened, he only heard two feet, not four.

Sam got closer so he could hear better. That was when he

bumped into Ophelia. Ophelia thought that Sam was a rat because he was on the ground, running quickly, like rats do. Sam thought Ophelia was Venus, so he jumped on her.

"Ahh!" Ophelia yelled, and they recognized each other.

Sam felt embarrassed because he had pounced on a girl, not a cat. He thought she would yell at him or make fun of him. Just then, Sam saw his cat behind Ophelia. Venus was laying down being lazy, away from the water.

Meanwhile, Professor Scalious was in the other tunnel, and heard a big bump. Then he heard Ophelia and Sam talking. He raced out of his tunnel and went in after them. Professor Scalious came up from under the water and tried to speak. Sam recognized the lizard's big, old eyes. Then Sam told Ophelia and Venus to hop on Scalious's back.

Ophelia bonked Professor Scalious on the head with a torch and he turned back to normal size.

"UGH!" said Scalious.

"I'll get you next. I'll eat you, Scalious!" Venus said quietly in a hungry voice to Scalious. Because Scalious was kind of small again, Venus wanted to eat him again.

Sam, Ophelia, Venus, and Scalious decided to go back through the tunnel to the island. Sam didn't want to leave without his treasure—he had found gold and silver and crystals and diamonds in the tunnel. He shared some with the others. He gave some to Professor Scalious so he could build his own yoga school. Ophelia got money for a new home for her brothers and sisters. Venus got a spa, to do whatever she wanted. And Sam was still going to be a plain old treasure hunter.

A CRACK DOWN
THE MIDDLE

ALEJANDRO PEREZ, GRADE 3

One night, Sam, Ophelia, and Professor Scalious were playing their favorite game, Pin-the-Tail-on-Ophelia. All of a sudden, Sam noticed that his island was moving. Before they could do anything there was a crack down the middle, and Ophelia and Professor

Scalious were stranded on the other side. Sam knew that if they didn't do something, the island would break in half!

"Jump to my side of the island," said Sam, but they were too scared to jump.

Then a volcano erupted, and the island moved even more. The crack was now as big as a hallway! "Now we should jump, so Sam won't be alone," Ophelia said to Professor Scalious.

"It's too wide to jump. I'll just have to build a bridge," said the lizard, and he started to build a bridge. It was hard work.

While they were building the bridge, the volcano erupted again. So they had to come up with another great idea. They began to think and think. Finally, Professor Scalious had an awesome idea. "I know what to build. We should build a wall out of sand castles and it should have a bridge, so Sam can pass to our side."

They built the sand castle wall all night, and in the morning, the island was fixed.

SOMETHING
REALLY WEIRD

BRITTANY MCPHERSON, GRADE 7

On the Brussels sprout farm, Sam's family had opened a supermarket that sold local fish, vegetables, and fruits. Sam's mom worked at the store while his dad caught the local fish in the nearby lake. Sam, however, had to pick the fruit and plant the vegetables and harvest them. Sam had very good street smarts and could trade eggs for milk or bread for their store.

One day, Sam went out with Venus to harvest the vegetables and pick the fruit. Venus started to scamper around and meow and then started to scratch Sam. Venus usually didn't scratch him, so Sam knew that something was wrong.

Sam asked, "Venus, why are you acting so weird? Just a few days ago, you were fine. What's wrong?"

But all Venus did was meow even more, so Sam continued to harvest the vegetables and pick the fruits to take back to his mother at the store.

The next morning, Sam and Venus did the usual routine, as they did every morning. When Sam went to pick the apples from the apple tree, the apples were all bruised and soft. Sam wondered what had happened overnight and why the apples were all bruised.

"Something is definitely up," thought Sam. "I need to talk to Scalious and Ophelia." He called them up and everyone agreed to meet on the farm after Ophelia was done with work.

"What is it?" Ophelia and the professor asked as soon as they saw Sam.

"Have you noticed that Venus has been acting really weird lately?"

"Yeah, we have." Professor Scalious told Sam. "Did you know

that she came by the lab the other day trying to get our attention while we were working on our invention?"

"The fruit, something really weird is happening to the fruit. Just come with me to my parent's store. I'll show you."

When they walked into the store to go to the back, they saw Venus sitting in the middle of the aisle by the magazine rack. Venus had knocked over the rack and pushed several of the magazines

 open. When Sam bent down to put them back, he read what Venus had spelled out across the pages: **THE ISLAND** in bold letters, and **IS IN DANGER**.

Sam called Professor Scalious and Ophelia over to look at the magazines. Ophelia, Sam, and the professor all stared at one another with curious looks and ran out of the store!

SAVING THE ISLAND

JOVAN ALDUEN, GRADE 6

"Oh no! My island is moving!" screamed Sam. "Professor Scalious, you have to help me."

"Maybe we should dive under the water and see what's causing the island to move," Professor Scalious said.

"That could be dangerous," Ophelia pointed out.

"This is our *island*! We have to do what it takes. And look, the island is moving away from the shore!"

The three friends got ready to dive. Professor Scalious used to go diving for fish, so he showed them how to do it. Under the water, they saw orange- and white-striped fish, and then, bubbling water rising up from the bottom. It was an active underwater volcano, black with hot red lava trying to escape from holes on the bottom. Sam was shocked. They had been sure the volcano was done erupting!

Professor Scalious was surprised, too, but he was thinking like a scientist. He swam closer to the volcano to get a look at the bottom. He knew if he could find a strong spot to place a hook, he could keep the island from moving. One of the holes with the hot red lava would be perfect for this.

When he was done exploring, Professor Scalious signaled to his friends to swim back up to shore with him. They got there, and he said, "Let's go back to the laboratory. We need to build some grappling hooks from the metal I have there. Then we can keep the island from moving by attaching one end to the ground, and one end to the volcano."

"I really love this island, so I'll try anything," agreed Sam.

Ophelia said, "I'm scared the volcano is going to erupt, but you're my friends, and I'll always help you with any situation."

Professor Scalious, Sam, and Ophelia raced to the laboratory where they used special gloves to twist the metal into hooks. Then they put an extra layer of non-melting metal on the outside, to protect the hooks from the lava. They squeezed the rest of the metal into a rope to tie between the hooks.

As they were working, Sam said, "At least the island will stay in one place with these grappling hooks. If only we knew the volcano wouldn't erupt."

"I think this is going to work," Ophelia stated enthusiastically.

When they were finished with the grappling hooks and the holding rope, they put everything into place. Professor Scalious and Sam bravely swam down to put the grappling hooks into the holes of the volcano. Ophelia and Venus dug the other end into the ground of the island. It worked!

Everyone gathered back on the shore, and Sam said, "Thank you guys, for helping me stop the island from floating away!"

PART 5

IN OUTER SPACE

THE ROCKET SHIP

ALEXIS GARCIA-SANCHEZ, GRADE 2

One day after the island was saved, Sam, Venus, Ophelia, and Professor Scalious were in their cardboard house reading a book about outer space and the stars. There were pictures about spaceships that were gray, and their bottoms were red with fire.

Sam said, "I think we should go to space!"

Ophelia said, "I think so, too!"

Professor Scalious asked, "What would we wear? And how are we going to get a spaceship?"

They went to Ophelia's factory and got 100 pieces of cardboard and started to build the spaceship outside of the cardboard factory. Then, they painted it with gray and red paint and named it the

"Gray/Red Spaceship!" They used what they had found around the factory to help the spaceship fly. Then, they used fire to get the spaceship going.

Ophelia, Sam, and Professor Scalious put things inside the spaceship to help it move up and down and land. They brought bread with peanut butter to make

sandwiches and juice to drink. They also brought strawberries for dessert. They all got in the rocket ship through the door that Professor Scalious helped build.

Inside the rocket ship there was a lot of room! Venus hopped in at the last minute before takeoff. They were all dressed in space clothes that looked like superheroes on TV.

Sam said, "5, 4, 3, 2, 1—GO!"

They flew the spaceship around outer space. As they looked out the windows, Sam saw a planet with rings!

As they flew on, Professor Scalious said, "There's Pluto."

Sam said, "It looks like a star."

Venus was scared because she thought the stars were ghosts.

ALIEN PLANET

AMYAH ORTEGA, TYLER OSBEY, AND BELICIA VEGA, GRADE 2

Ophelia, Sam, and Professor Scalious landed on Alien Planet. As they got off the spaceship, they were greeted by fire aliens, guitar-headed aliens, and poison aliens. The aliens took them to the alien store. Sam and Ophelia got to sketch out an alien they wanted. They put their drawings into the slot of the alien machine

and the machine made a guitar-strum noise and suddenly two baby aliens came out for Sam and Ophelia to take home.

After the alien store, the three friends went to go eat alien pizza. The alien pizza had a green crust with green cheese, green peppers, red sauce, and purple potato chips. Everybody tasted it, and it tasted good at first, but then kind of nasty after they chewed it. They decided to feed it to the baby aliens.

When Sam and Ophelia went to the clothing store to get clothes for their new aliens, they ran into Venus. Venus wanted to go on to the planet Venus, so they boarded the spaceship and headed off.

When exploring the planet Venus, they found a big hole. They wanted to explore it, except they heard something strange behind them so they turned around and started walking backward. Suddenly, Professor Scalious, Sam, Ophelia, and Venus felt something pulling on them, and, before they knew it, they got sucked into the crater. As they fell in, they got stuck in a stew of alien spider webs and the baby aliens ran off!

As Venus clawed everyone out of the spider webs the baby aliens flew off into space. Ophelia and Venus realized that luckily Sam hadn't been sucked into the crater. Sam told them to make a human rope, but it wasn't long enough, so they used the webs to extend the rope. They threw the rope up to the edge of the crater to Sam, who caught it and hooked it onto a rock. Ophelia climbed up first, then Venus and Professor Scalious hooked tails and climbed out, too.

KIDNAPPED BY THE ALIENS

ISAAC BERNAL, EHAB DAHBOUR, AND CYNTHIA RAUDALES-ZAVALA, GRADE 3

Sam woke up later than usual. Normally, he'd be woken up by Ophelia's incredibly loud snoring, which echoed through the spaceship halls like a T. Rex stomping on the floor. But this time, he didn't hear a sound. He got out of bed and crept over to the kitchen to have some Spacer-ade Energy Drink for breakfast. He noticed something odd, though. There was a note on the refrigerator, which read:

SAM, I LEFT. I'LL BE BACK IN A CUPPLE OF WEEKS. —OPHELIA
P.S. DON'T COME LOOCKING FOR ME. I'M OKAY.

Sam was utterly speechless and dropped his drink, which floated off into the air. He thought to himself, "Why would she just leave like that without telling me? I'm her best friend!" Then he noticed that the note was all slimy and her spelling was suspiciously wrong, like an alien's bad handwriting and poor spelling.

"Oh no! I know what's going on. Ophelia's been kidnapped by the aliens!" he cried.

Sam was terrified. He knew the aliens' reputation and he knew they weren't to be messed with. He called on the one lizard he knew could handle the crisis: Professor Scalious.

In two light-flashes, Scalious appeared at the portal door, sweating and looking worried. "I'm gonna get them!" he instantly yelled. "They're gonna pay the consequences for taking her right from under us!" Before Sam could even talk to him, Scalious was already loading up his laser gear and a star-gun for a serious rescue mission. The star-gun was his own personal invention and his calling card. When it zapped someone, the beam instantly turned him or her into a star forever and ever.

"Come on, what are you waiting for?!" Scalious yelled at Sam.

"Um, I'm TERRIFIED! Aren't you?!"

"Don't worry, I've done this before. If we're a team, everything will work out just fine, and we'll have Ophelia home in no time," Scalious assured him.

Sam took a second and thought over their options, but knew what had to be done.

He turned to Scalious and gave him a nod.

"Let's roll!" Scalious yelled.

They loaded up into their tiny Space Jet and undocked from the station as quickly as they could. Scalious instantly picked up a familiar scent. "That's the advantage of being lizard, my friend," Scalious said. "I'm picking up their slimy scent right now, and it's leading us that way." He pointed the ship's coordinates to EAST.

The aliens had done a sloppy job hiding their trail from a lizard, because in no time, the group was entering the Green Planet's airspace.

"Why do they call it that?" Sam asked.

"What?" Scalious responded, at the helm of the controls.

"The Green Planet. Why do they call it 'Green Planet'?"

"You see, they call it that because it's shaped like a dollar sign and is completely made of slime. Also, that ring you see around the planet, look here."

At that moment, Scalious pulled down the telescope and zoomed in on the Green Planet's outer ring.

"The ring is all filled with gold coins and rocks shaped like dollar signs!" Sam yelled.

As they approached the Green Planet, Sam realized he'd packed the radar that Ophelia left in her room. "Wait, I forgot! I brought Ophelia's radar!" Sam yelled out. He whipped out the homemade device and turned it on. But there was no sound.

"Oh no, it isn't picking her up!" Sam said. Then all of a sudden it started beeping like a sped-up piano.

"Where does it say she is?" Scalious asked.

"Wait this doesn't make sense," Sam responded. "It says they're right on top of us! How's that possible?!"

Then they looked up and yelled together, "Oh no!"

From their bay window, they saw the Alien Mother ship right above them. And in the front window of the spaceship, they saw the

Head Alien holding Ophelia hostage, tied up with snakes in a rat pit.

Scalious noticed with his eagle-like vision that there was a nearly invisible string linked to a booby trap, connected to a rock. They realized it was a trap. Before they could do anything, their portal door opened and they saw a galactic force boarding their spaceship with Ophelia tied up behind them, screaming.

"We've been waiting for wou," the Head Alien said calmly to Sam and Scalious, as the Alien Guards tied them up. "Wou fell wight into our twap."

"Give her back, you monster!" Scalious yelled out.

"What do you want from us?" Sam asked nervously.

"We want the Pwofessor, of course. We want to expand our empire...to Earth! And he's the only one of wus who knows how to get there!"

"I'm not one of you! I'd NEVER be one of you!" Scalious yelled.

"Are wou sure about that?" the Head Alien said, smirking.

Sam realized he still had his star-gun in his back pocket, which the Guards had forgotten to check. He slowly moved his eyes around the room, sizing up his options.

"All we want is for wou to take us to Earth, and we'll give back the girl. It's as easy and shimple as that," the Alien said.

"I have an idea," Scalious said. "How about I just take my friend and zap you into the slime that you came from, you weed."

The Head Alien just smiled and worked his way back to Ophelia. He put his slimy face right next to hers and she twisted her face in disgust. She spat in his face and kicked him, and he stumbled.

At that moment, Sam saw a window of opportunity. He kicked the star-gun out from his back pocket and Scalious grabbed it from the air. He aimed it right at the Head Alien and zapped him.

A huge ray of light exploded out of the star-gun and turned him into a supernova. Just as Sam and Scalious got over to free

Ophelia from her snake-ropes, the supernova collapsed and turned into a black hole. It started sucking all the aliens in, including the Head Alien.

Sam and Professor Scalious carried Ophelia on their backs toward their ship controls, and kicked the remaining aliens off the open door. They closed up everything before it could suck them in, too, and warped back to their spaceship to safety.

"Are you okay?" Sam asked Ophelia, cradling her in his arms.

"My mouth tastes like snakes!" Ophelia said, smiling. "But otherwise, I'm fine. I really need a shower, though."

Scalious took a whiff of her hair. "Yeah, you do!" he joked.

The next morning, Sam woke up earlier than he had wanted, because of a loud snoring sound roaring through the ship. Instead of yelling, he just got back into bed and smiled.

PITHOLYA

GABRIEL HURTADO, GRADE 2

On their way back from space, Sam, Ophelia, and Professor Scalious flew to a planet called Pitholya. When they landed, they saw that there were flying cars everywhere with space animals driving. There was a lion with six eyes and eight legs, and instead of tiny lizards there were giant lizards that were bigger than dinosaurs. Scalious was a bit jealous. He thought, "If I lived here I would be as big as them, but unfortunately I don't live here."

When Ophelia, Sam, and Professor Scalious got out of the spaceship they saw IHOPs everywhere. They learned that Pitholya had billions of IHOPs—and every day another million were built! They wanted so many because the aliens on Pitholya loved pancakes, eggs, and sausages.

The three friends stopped for a minute and worried that since there were so many IHOPs it could be a trap and the food could be poisonous. But Ophelia was really curious, really hungry, and she loved IHOPs.

"On the sign it says everything is free," she said. "It might not be poisonous. It might be so good they want to give it away!"

They went inside an IHOP and saw animals walking on two legs. They asked a waiter, "Is everything free?"

"Of course," he answered. "Why do you think there is a sign out there that says that?"

So they ordered a meal and started to eat. Ophelia loved everything that was there—she got pancakes with syrup, chocolate chips, and butter. Sam also got pancakes with chocolate chips.

Professor Scalious got a fish omelet.

"Not bad," said Scalious.

"I guess it's okay," Sam agreed.

They finished their meal and went right to bed because they were so tired from traveling. That night, they all had crazy dreams that their rocket was an IHOP.

The next day they went to eat breakfast at another IHOP. Everyone ordered banana milkshakes to celebrate their new planet discovery.

"Sorry, no bananas," said the waiter.

"What do you mean?" cried Ophelia. She was angry.

The waiter felt sorry and explained that they were all gone. Millions were stolen by thirty gorillas. "We probably won't see them again," he said.

But the three friends *really* wanted banana milkshakes, so they decided to save the day. The waiter told them about the Gorilla Factory down south where gorillas worked three million hours a day. Each second they made more than ten million bananas.

Ophelia, Sam, and Professor Scalious went to find the factory and when they got there they asked the gorillas why they had stolen the bananas.

"The only thing we do is work, work, work and we never get to *eat* any of the bananas!" said the head gorilla.

"Well, that doesn't sound fun," said Sam.

They had to take the bananas back to IHOP and the gorillas were still in trouble because on that planet they had lots of rules on good behavior. But Ophelia, Sam, and Professor Scalious were able to take the gorillas to a really nice zoo that would let them have some bananas. It was a new property.

"Thanks!" said the gorillas.

The three friends delivered the rest of the stolen bananas back to IHOP and finally had milkshakes.

"How did you figure out where they were?" asked the waiter.

Professor Scalious said, "You told us where to go, and all we had to do was ask nicely."

PART 6

SAVING PROFESSOR SCALIOUS

When Sam, Ophelia, and Professor Scalious returned to earth. Professor Scalious published his scientific findings in several journals, and won another Amateur Scientist's Choice Award. Best of all, he was granted an honorary degree by the town's university— no small thing for a lizard-scientist! The ceremony was set to take place on New Year's Eve, and as Scalious prepared for the big event, he could hardly contain himself. He had no idea what lay in store for him.

PROFESSOR SCALIOUS

KARINA MORALES, GRADE 6

It was a huge day for Stephen Scalious. He was in the hardest yoga position you can ever think of and of course writing a poem. It was the day of his graduation to become a *real* professor of science! Just when he was writing the last line of his poem, Venus came over and said, "Hey Stephen, care to join me for dinner?" Stephen quickly imagined himself on a plate with an apple in his mouth in the middle of a table with Venus sitting at the other end holding a fork and knife.

Just as Venus was going to grab him, Stephen slipped on his red scale-soothing shoes and ran as fast as he could to the university. He checked his watch and noticed he was late. He also noticed that his red scale-soothing shoes were dirty! Meanwhile, Venus kept chasing Stephen, until she got distracted by a FREE MICE sign.

"Good thing I put that sign there yesterday!" Stephen said, huffing loudly. Running across the street, he dove through a hole in a fence and landed right in front of the school. Finally, Stephen had arrived at his graduation. Everybody was already there. His name was the next to be called. He checked his shoes to see if they were still dirty and realized that he wasn't wearing his robe! He forgot to put it on after yoga! At this point he was panicking and standing in his own pool of sweat. He had to go up without his robe, wearing only his dirty red shoes.

Once he saw Sam and Ophelia smiling up at him from the crowd, he stopped sweating pools. He felt much more confident than before. He levitated up to the microphone in lotus position and announced, "Thank you for giving me this diploma. I'm sorry you had to see me like this, but I've got to go finish my poem now."

The crowd was surprised to see a naked lizard walk across the stage for his diploma, but he didn't care. Stephen had finally truly become Professor Scalious.

THE PLAN

JUSTIN JOHNSON, GRADE 8

January 1, 12:02 a.m.

"I, Professor William Harold James Boogledorf III, am the greatest scientist the world has ever seen. There is no fact that

I don't know! Yet, they give my award to this Professor Scalious. Outrage, I tell you, outrage! I shall not let this deed go unpunished. I will see to it that by the end of the month I will have thrown cake in his face once more," Boogledorf said.

"Don't get so worked up," said the young scientist Woun Williams. "You know you have high blood pressure."

"Be silent, boy," said Boogledorf. "I am constantly having to clean up your messes. Ugh."

"You can't pick your family members."

Woun Williams was Boogledorf's incredibly annoying grandson. They'd never really seen eye-to-eye since he refused to change his last name to Boogledorf. Instead, he chose to keep Williams.

"Get out!" yelled Boogledorf.

"It's my house," said Woun.

"Don't remind me," said Boogledorf. "I mean, really—pink bunnies on the wall? 1970's lava lamps? You call this a house? It doesn't even have a *TV*. How am I

supposed to watch my show about a guy watching a show?"

"So, how are you going to capture Scalious?" chuckled Williams. "Throw cake at him?"

"Really?" said Boogledorf, annoyed. "Are you mocking the power of cake-in-face?"

"No, sir," said Williams. "But how are you?"

"Easy," said Boogledorf. "I will lure him to an alley without his friends. Hit him in the face with two cakes. One of which will have strawberries, which he is highly allergic to. His face will swell up, then I'll wrap him with my pet snake and put him in a box."

"Won't Humphrey bite Scalious?" said Williams. Humphrey

was a black and white snake. He loved to roll around in jelly and eat pillows.

"Only if I give the command," said Boogledorf.

"So when does the plan start?" said Williams anxiously.

"When you buy a TV!"

WHO TURNED OFF THE LIGHTS?

MAKAYLA BRADFORD, GRADE 5

While Sam, Ophelia, and Professor Scalious were having a party to celebrate the professor's graduation, they discovered they needed more chips and dip. Professor Scalious was the nicest lizard in the world so he went across the lake to the nearest store he could find. While he was walking, the streetlights cut off. Even the store lights went off. He was kind of scared because it was really dark. His lizard heart was beating so quickly that you could hear it from a mile away. He started walking really fast because the store was pretty far—five blocks away. He could barely see the sign. He was walking down a dark, creepy city street. Nobody was around.

"Don't be nervous, don't be nervous! Just walk, just walk!" he said to himself. He kept walking forward. Suddenly, he heard a snake behind him: "Ssss!"

"Ssss!"

A voice said, "Did you know that if you chew gum when you cut up onions, you don't cry?"

The voice sounded squeaky and creaky.

"Uh-oh." Professor Scalious knew this meant trouble.

He started to run toward the island for help. He was running as fast as he could, but he heard something really fast behind him.

Professor Scalious spied an alley with a trashcan and hid slowly. He peered behind him...suddenly, under a streetlight, he saw an old man with a snake wrapped around his body. The man had very pale skin and bright blue, glow-in-the-dark eyes. His teeth looked terrible and his hair looked even worse. He seemed like he was eight feet tall because Professor Scalious was so short.

"Honey is so easy to digest," the man said in a creaky voice. "You know why? Because it's already been digested by bees!" His deep, dark voice sounded like he was using a microphone.

The snake started slithering toward Professor Scalious, who began to panic.

He screeched, "Why meeeee!!" in his tiny voice. He knew he couldn't get away from this guy. Professor Scalious would be captured no matter what he tried. Professor Scalious was screaming like a little girl at a concert. The snake wrapped around and it all went black.

"Who turned off the lights?" asked Professor Scalious.

THE DISCOVERY

MELINDA HERNANDEZ, GRADE 6

Two hours later, Sam and Ophelia noticed that Professor Scalious was still gone. At first they thought he might have stopped by a friend's house, but when time went by and they still didn't hear anything, they thought something was wrong. They got on the phone and started calling around, but couldn't find him anywhere. Ophelia got off the phone and urgently said, "This is useless. I'm going to go out and try to find him."

She took a flashlight, a bag with her cell phone in case Sam called, and a phone book to keep calling people just in case.

"That doesn't sound safe," Sam said calmly. "I don't think that's a smart idea. It's already night outside and civilization is a dangerous world."

"Professor Scalious is family, and family is *family*, so I have to go. I'll be back later and I'll call you if I find anything."

Without saying another word, Ophelia left the island.

Once Ophelia got to shore, the first place she looked was the shortcut that Professor Scalious always took. It started off at the shore and it went through a few side streets and then into an alley. The alley was dark and Ophelia felt something in her stomach. She always got this weird feeling in her stomach when something bad was about to happen. She walked down the alley cautiously making sure she tried to get every clue she could find. At the end of the alley, she found the lizard's favorite scarf. It had blue and green stripes with the words "Best Lizard on Earth" on it. It was a Christmas gift from Ophelia and Sam. Ophelia knew Scalious would never leave that on purpose. She began to feel scared and unsafe. She quickly went back to the island to tell Sam what she had found.

She found Sam talking on the phone with a close relative and he was quivering by this time. By now it had been thirty more minutes. She motioned for him to get off the phone so she could tell him what she found. When he hung up, she came running up to him, talking so fast he couldn't understand.

"Slow down! Slow down!" Sam said. "Tell me what happened!"

When Ophelia slowed down, she began to explain what she found and the images that flashed in her head.

"And I was so scared!" she cried. "I knew something was going to happen. I got that weird feeling in my stomach."

Sam was pacing back and forth and playing with his hands and kind of nervous.

Together they went back to shore and went into the alley. Using a flashlight, they finally found it—a squished chocolate cake and half a cup of coffee smashed against the dumpster. Sam was the first to see it. He quickly called Ophelia over and right away she shouted, "I know what happened to Scalious! Boogledorf stole our poor lizard! But where can we find him?"

Just then, they noticed something else. Under an old bed sheet in the alley they saw the corner of what they thought was a pillowcase. But when they went to examine it, they realized it was actually a blueprint. It was a blueprint of a secret laboratory underground! The blueprint had spilt coffee and frosting-coated fingerprints on the corners. They both stood quietly for five minutes, thinking the same thing. Ophelia was the first to shout out her thought. "This can lead us in  the right direction. It must be where he took Professor Scalious!"

Sam said, "I have an old friend that used to be close with Boogledorf when he was still a good guy." Sam quickly opened the phonebook and dialed his friend Martha. He said slowly, so she could understand him, "Do you know anything about an underground laboratory?"

Martha stayed quiet for a few moments, like she was being careful with what she was saying. She started off stuttering, and then it all came clear.

When the phone call ended, Ophelia and Sam knew just what to do and just where to go. They went back to their island and prepared for a serious adventure. They were ready.

AN IMPASSIONED SPEECH BY PROFESSOR STEPHEN SCALIOUS

GRACE ANDRE, GRADE 7

People, people! i'm a lizard, for crying out loud. i'm no use to this villain. Although, if this villain doesn't let me go i'm going to have to put my mind to work. i've got some tricks up my scales and i'm not afraid to use them. i could easily

attack him. i could hide until Boogledorf can't find me or i could teach him yoga and then he would fall asleep so i could escape. See, for example, i could easily pounce on this stupid villain and go crazy on him. i could use my surroundings to create a diversion to distract the villain. i can use what i learned from all my reading to conjure up an experiment. i'm not afraid to get down and dirty. no super-villain should ever come near me thinking i'm going to be all peachy with him kidnapping me. no way, josé! you do that and you're officially being put on my bad list.

I can act like everything's okay, but really i'm freaking out that maybe I could be eaten. I mean, I do look quite tasty, don't you think? or possibly be held hostage forever and no one would come looking for me! Trust me, I can't take living with this cranky old man, william Harold James Boogledorf iii. I mean, whoever heard of such a stupid name like that? His parents probably shipped him off somewhere so he could bother someone else with his useless facts about bananas and such. And I've gotten hit with about twenty strawberry cakes already! I hate strawberries. I'd like to throw one big fat cake at his wrinkly face and see how he likes it.

Let me tell you, since I've been trapped in here all I want to do is sleep, but no! I'm woken up everyday by the most annoying and obnoxious noise ever: Boogledorf slurping his coffee. He slurps coffee ten times louder than ophelia snores. I wish I had some coffee so I could put that fat old grump in his place. This is why i'm asking any of my friends to help me. please! I don't want to be trapped here. Everything that goes on here with Boogledorf is seriously driving me mad. For now, don't worry about me. I can hold my own ground — just hurry up!

SAVING PROFESSOR SCALIOUS

VIVIANA DE ALBA, GRADE 2

Ophelia and Sam were scared. As they snuck into Boogledorf's underground laboratory to save Professor Scalious, they weren't sure if it would just be Boogledorf or an entire group of evil sidekicks. Ophelia wasn't that scared though. She had been working on plans ever since Scalious turned up missing and she thought it would be easy to save him.

"Let's look around," whispered Ophelia. "Maybe there's something here to disguise ourselves with."

They saw the doorway to Scalious being guarded by some bad guys and a leopard. Sam and Ophelia decided to be chameleons. They got this trick from Professor Scalious—he was always trying to be a chameleon.

The guards were wearing yellow and dark colors and leather cloaks, but all Sam and Ophelia could find to make their costumes were orange and pink clothes.

"Ophelia...I don't know about this," said Sam. "What if this plan doesn't work? Do you have another plan?"

"Relax," said Ophelia. "It will work." And it almost did. The friends snuck up to the guards and Sam interrupted and said, "Boogledorf said we could guard Scalious. You guys can go."

Ophelia—who was sometimes a showoff—got a little mad that Sam's idea was better than hers, but she went along with it.

They started to head to where Scalious was. But just then, the head guard noticed Venus's tail sticking out from under Sam's cloak.

"Wait a minute!" said the guard. He turned to his friends and said, "Go to Boogledorf and tell him they are here."

The leopard who was with the bad guys had a secret camera on his collar that showed Boogledorf a picture of what was going on.

"It's them!" he yelled when he saw Venus's tail. "Oh my gosh, it's the same cat! They're trying to take Professor Scalious!"

Ophelia, Sam, and Venus had no idea they were being followed. Boogledorf rushed down after them with the other guards.

"Run! Run!" Ophelia yelled.

"I told you this plan wouldn't work!" said Sam.

"It would have if it weren't for your cat!"

But there wasn't any more time to argue. Boogledorf had cornered them.

"Go get them!" he told the guards. It didn't look good for Sam and Ophelia.

Just then, Ophelia had one more great idea. As usual, she had three spare cardboard boxes on her. She had used them at work one day and her boss told her, "Make sure you put those back when you're done," but she forgot. She had kept them ever since then because you never know when a cardboard box will come in handy.

Ophelia said, "You go, Sam. I'll take care of this."

She quickly built a cardboard wall and tossed a box over it. It landed right on Boogledorf's head.

"Somebody take this off my head!" yelled Boogledorf.

"Never! See you in jail, Boogledorf!"

Ophelia ran to catch up with Sam. They were going to save Scalious.

THE ESCAPE

BRENNEN BARISO, GRADE 7

By then, Sam had turned a corner and was sprinting down the hall. He looked behind him and saw Ophelia and Venus running to catch up with him. He wordlessly motioned for them to follow him, and they quickly entered a supply closet and shut the door.

As they sat in the darkness, they could hear the stampede of footsteps passing by them and the unmistakable sound of Boogledorf's voice yelling, "Hurry up and catch them! They can't have gotten too far! The human eyeball never grows!"

When Sam and Ophelia both decided it was safe to exit, they slowly opened the closet door and stepped out into the hallway. Ophelia led the way as the trio backtracked to the door which used to be heavily guarded. They knew that behind that door was their friend, Professor Scalious.

"How am I supposed to open this door?" Sam asked, turning to look at a puzzled Ophelia and a determined Venus.

"Should we push it?" Ophelia had her shoulder pressed up against the door, shoving with all her might, but the door just wouldn't budge. Suddenly, Sam was struck with an idea.

"Shhhhh," he said, motioning for Ophelia to stand back. Sam leaned in close to the grey, steel door with no obvious way to open it.

"I. Hate. Wisconsin," Sam said aloud, hoping he was right. There was a deafening silence as Sam's hope started to fade, but then a clear *click* was heard coming from the door and it slid soundlessly open. He had guessed the password!

"We're in." Ophelia's eyes beamed and her words were accompanied by a contented meow from Venus, as if to make sure she wasn't forgotten by her friends.

The trio stepped into the dimly lit room and spotted a box sitting on a low table off to the side. Other than the one piece of furniture, the room was barren. Ophelia, rushing over to the box—which she was sure contained her lizard friend—ripped open the top, but she had to hold in her gasp as she saw Scalious being trapped by a large black and white snake.

"Look," Ophelia said as Sam stepped closer and Venus jumped

up on the table to get a closer look.

"Oh, finally!" Scalious winked at his friends as the snake surrounding him started to snore, obviously asleep. "I thought you might never come!"

"Scalious! Are you alright?" Sam asked, carefully peeling down the sides of the box so that Scalious didn't have to crane his neck up from the snake to see them.

"Of course I'm alright. Not even Boogledorf could break my spirit. Now, it's really just my pal the snake right here that's the problem."

"Well, how would you recommend we get rid of that problem, Scalious?" Ophelia said, fumbling with a spare piece of cardboard from her pocket. She stepped back in order to try and see the situation from a different perspective, but to no avail.

Before Scalious could answer Ophelia, Venus decided to take up her friend's challenge and bit the snake surrounding Scalious on its tail.

The snake suddenly awoke and unwrapped itself from the lizard it was holding captive, and quickly started to chase after Venus, who at this point in time, had scurried out the door.

"Venus, wait!" Sam yelled after his cat, but the snake followed her out the door and into the hallway.

"Don't worry, Sam. Venus will be fine. She's a smart cat," Ophelia said, taking Scalious up into her palm. She knew that Venus would find her way back to them, but she wasn't exactly thinking about that—she was just happy to have her friend back from the hands of Boogledorf.

Sam was eager to rescue his cat from the snake and leave Boogledorf's house as quickly as possible. Pulling Ophelia at his side, the three of them started to walk through the hallways in the direction they were sure they had seen Venus run off in. From up above, Scalious could hear the stomping of the boots worn by Boogledorf's comrades.

Boogledorf had given up trying to find Sam and Ophelia, and ordered everyone to go back to their posts guarding Scalious. Sam, knowing that at any second they could come face-to-face with Boogledorf, quickly changed directions and rounded the corner leading to a staircase they hoped would take them out of the laboratory. Next to it, laid the same black and white snake that was chasing Venus; it was now resting, simply because its body was too thick to even climb the first step. Just as Ophelia was reaching the stairs, Boogledorf and his minions burst out of the doorway leading to the stairs opposite of Sam.

"There they are!" Boogledorf yelled and added, "Men are more likely than women to be left-handed!" He burst into a run to catch up with Ophelia. Sam sprinted up the stairs, passing by the black and white snake slumbering right next to the bottom step. Sam, Ophelia, and Scalious ran all the way up to ground level, where they found Venus but no door to escape. They kept climbing until they reached the third floor of Boogledorf's house. Below them, Ophelia heard the sound of Boogledorf and his minions tripping over the snoring snake.

Sam knew that Boogledorf and his minions were coming up the stairs and were getting close, so he had to act quickly. Grabbing the thick fabric cord from the drapes to his right, Sam fashioned a makeshift tightrope. Ophelia sensed what Sam was planning to do and opened up the window. Both of them knew they were running out of time.

Tying a knot on the end of the rope, Sam threw the tightrope into the branches of the tree right outside the window, catching it on several prickly twigs.

"C'mon, Venus," Sam said as he stepped out of the window onto the tightrope without hesitation, along with his cat, Venus. Ophelia didn't worry, as she knew that Sam had a secret talent of tightrope walking.

When the two of them reached the oak tree—with Venus scurrying along—they stepped out onto its sturdy limbs. Untangling the tightrope from the mixture of leaves and twigs, Sam let it fall so that it ran along the length of Boogledorf's house. Sam winked at Ophelia and Scalious, although he wasn't sure she could see him.

Seeing Boogledorf and his company appear at the end of the hallway, Ophelia let Scalious hop into her shirt pocket and she jumped out of the window, scaling the house down to the ground by gripping the same rope Sam had just walked on a few moments ago.

"Let's go!" Scalious yelled as Sam snatched up Venus and they ran as quickly as they could away from Boogledorf's house, feeling victorious. In the distance, they heard him calling after them, "Children laugh 400 times a day!"

It was Ophelia's idea to walk through the bushes on the way back to Sam's island, just to make sure they weren't being followed. It didn't take a long time to reach the canoe, and the whole gang jumped in and rowed to the island, where they knew they were safe once and for all from Boogledorf.

EPILOGUE

Hey, you, reader! You may wonder what happened to our characters after Professor Scalious got his diploma. Well, when Professor Scalious was doing a science project, he messed up... again. There was a good side of this big mistake, though, because his failed experiment made another island right next to Sam's island. And now the three friends are living on it and have their own business: a Brussels sprouts/inventions/science production lab. Anyone can find something they want there.

They are all business partners. Professor Scalious is the one who deals with all the science projects, because now that he has his diploma, people give him free supplies. Sam is the one who deals with all the Brussels sprouts. He still doesn't like Brussels sprouts, but he knew a lot about them, so he figured, "Why not? I guess I'll just stick with them—but only if I don't have to eat them." Ophelia is the one who is the inventor in the business. She now has her own office and it's the size of the Empire State Building. It's a lot of space and she can think more freely there. She spends much time in there, and comes out with great ideas.

Their favorite part of working together is that the three get to have each other as friends and traveling partners. That's right, they still travel. When they're not working—and sometimes even when they are—they continue to travel all over the universe in search of new creatures that can talk and love adventure just like them. They dream of going to a pink planet one day, but only one creature has ever done this: the pink ant. You might have heard of him before. When they aren't traveling or working, they still go to Sam's island, where they hang out, go scuba diving, and go to underground hotels.

When Sam, Ophelia, and Professor Scalious think about their adventures, they feel confident about themselves and are enjoying their journey in the world. They've learned that you can never have too many friends, but you can also never have too few friends—unless you don't have any. One good friend is always enough. Or in their case, two—and a cat. (And sometimes, an arch nemesis.)

When the three friends talk about their plans for the future, they know they will always have new experiences. Whether it's because of Professor Scalious's potions, Ophelia's inventions, or Sam's courageous spirit, their story is far from over...

Write Your Own Adventure about Sam, Ophelia, and Professor Scalious!

AUTHOR:
....

....

....

....

....

....

....

....

....

....

....

....

....

....

....

....

....

....

....

....

ABOUT THE AUTHORS

AMINE AHMEDYAHIA would like you to know that his favorite animal is the badger. *Belding, Mrs. Nelson's seventh grade*

COBY AKINS doesn't like sitting around. He'd rather be playing sports and jumping off of stuff. He also likes to draw cartoon characters and made-up things. His friends say he is funny. *Diego, Ms. Rasgus's sixth grade*

JOVAN ALDUEN would like to be a policeman when he grows up. He really likes to sing, especially songs by Michael Jackson and Chris Brown. *Diego, Ms. Zavala's sixth grade*

EMILY ALVARADO is from Chicago. When she grows up, she would like to be a singer. She has a brother named Alfredo. *Locke, Mrs. Alcantar's third grade*

JAMES ANDERSEN III has one brother and one sister. He feels good about them. *Locke, Ms. Ruiz's third grade*

GRACE ANDRE likes to read a lot—especially mysteries. When she is not reading, she enjoys running track. Grace also loves monkeys because they have such big ears. *Belding, Mrs. Nelson's seventh grade*

MAXIM ANDRIYCHUK was born in the Ukraine and is an only child. He's ten years old and when he grows up, he is going to be a scientist—this dream inspired his story in the book. *Erie, Ms. DeVooght's fourth grade*

BABY ANTUNEZ likes to eat chicken wings for dinner sometimes. She also loves to play soccer. *Tonti, Mrs. Dussias-Cuevas' third grade*

SHAKIYAH ASPHY always argues with her youngest sister but she gets over it. One time, she threw a ball at her sister and her sister fell on the floor. They both laughed about it. This incident inspired Shakiyah to write her story because she loves her sisters and brothers and likes telling other people the funny things they do. *Randolph, Ms. Lohitsa's sixth grade*

MIA BAEZ-VASQUEZ is nine years old and is bilingual. She has a dog named Roxanne. Mia loves writing and is considering being an author when she grows up. *Erie, Mr. Mitchell's fourth grade*

BRENNEN BARISO is very interested in becoming fluent in sign language and he also enjoys writing poetry in his spare time. Brennen's biggest goal in life is to publish a novel. *Thorp, seventh grade, 826CHI workshop*

EMILY BERMUDEZ is proud that her mother is from Puerto Rico and her father is from Costa Rica. When she grows up, Emily would like to be a vet because she loves animals. She has a white dog named Snow who looks like a poodle, even though he's a Bichon Frise. *Diego, Ms. Alexandroff's sixth grade*

ISAAC BERNAL says his favorite hobbies are playing video games and eating tasty foods. He likes to go to the park to play or swim— he can open his eyes underwater. On very hot days, Isaac has been known to drink as many as four bottles of water. *Locke, Ms. Ruiz's third grade*

EVA BERNATEK likes to read books from the A to Z Mysteries series. Her father used to be a policeman but now he's retired. Eva enjoys walking her dog Milo, even when he wants to chase squirrels and pulls the leash. *Pulaski, Mrs. Shane's second grade*

CAMERION BLAIR likes to play basketball because it's something he can express himself through, like art. He's an avid illustrator who especially likes drawing Vegeta, the action-packed hero on the show *Dragon Ball Z*. Someday, Camerion would like to see himself playing for the Chicago Bulls. *Drake, Mr. Coppola's eighth grade*

MAKAYLA BRADFORD has been to Louisiana five times. Her favorite part of these trips was going shopping for jewelry and some zucchini. *Burr, Mr. Patiño's fifth grade*

JOI BRADLEY has been writing for two years and only needs help spelling long words. She likes going to her grandma's to play with her cousins. They love to exercise, especially jump rope. *Erie, Ms. DeVooght's fourth grade*

SARAH BREINIG could have a long conversation about superheroes or history with pretty much anyone. She loves learning and also likes to doodle. *Home-schooled, sixth grade, 826CHI workshop*

LARONE BRIM, JR. likes to write fiction and likes to draw trees, mountains, and people. He learned his art skills from a painter on television and tried it out himself. Someday, Larone would like to create a cartoon or become a professional artist. *Peabody, Mr. Simpson's seventh grade*

JASON BROWN has five brothers and four sisters. His entire family went to Disney World last year. Jason really likes creative writing—though he's not crazy about the physical act of writing, he loves to make up stories. *Drake, Mr. Coppola's eighth grade*

MALIK BROWN is an undefeatable game legend and the best goalie you'll ever meet. His favorite book is *Milkweed* by Jerry Spinelli. *Peabody, Mr. Simpson's seventh grade*

ZAKARIA CHIHAB would like to be an action hero when he grows up. Also, he likes to ride his bike. *Belding, Mrs. Nelson's seventh grade*

SETH CORPUZ is originally from the Philippines. He likes to play video games and also soccer. He is a huge fan of the Chicago Fire Soccer Club. *Diego, Ms. Alexandroff's sixth grade*

VICTORIA CORTEZ is ten years old and is the smallest of all her siblings. She loves dogs. Victoria's favorite color is yellow. *Mitchell, Ms. Riefenberg's fourth grade*

MARTEZ CROSBY likes to play football. He is usually quiet and he likes poetry. *Harvard, Ms. Hemesath's eighth grade*

EHAB DAHBOUR likes video games and he also really likes math. When he grows up, Ehab would like to write books about things like history, action/adventure, life in the future, aliens, and forests. *Locke, Ms. Ruiz's third grade*

VIVIANA DE ALBA loves to go to the theater to watch movies with her family. She likes playing with her sister, and even lets her play with her stuffed animals. Some boys think girls like dolphins and kind animals—but Viviana likes tigers. *Pulaski, Mrs. Navarro's second grade*

CARLOS DIAZ loves gym and his favorite activity is playing with the parachute. Carlos would like to be a chef and he can cook things for people like eggs, pancakes, soup, lunch, and breakfast. *Mitchell, Ms. Riefenberg's fourth grade*

JADALYNNE GAGO-IZQUIERDO has more than fifty toys and is a proud member of Club Penguin! She's going to do some cool stuff when she grows up like be a businesswoman. *Pulaski, Mrs. Shane's second grade*

SAUL GARCIA once went camping in Michigan for two days. It was pretty awesome with all the blueberry fields and the other kids camping, too. Saul loves to build pillow forts with his younger brother and pillow fights until the forts collapse. *Erie, Mr. Mitchell's fourth grade*

ALEXIS GARCIA-SANCHEZ has family in Mexico and Michigan. She likes to play hide-and-seek and her favorite hiding spot is in her room because there is a lava lamp in it. *Pulaski, Ms. Meza's second grade*

NIA GIPSON thinks it is important to be creative because it's what brings people to the next level. She enjoys writing mysteries, science fiction, and narratives. Nia loves learning and hopes someday to combine her interests in law and children to become a criminal defense attorney. *Drake, Mr. Coppola's eighth grade*

SESASH GUTIERREZ lives in a very peaceful place where big kids sometimes play with little kids. *Tonti, Mrs. Kadow's fourth grade*

DIOVIONE HARRIS is smart and gets good grades. She also likes to go ice skating. One day, Diovionne had a dream that she was in Florida. She wants to go there someday. *Drake, Mrs. Bowen's fourth grade*

LORENZO HARRIS just got braces. So far he likes them, but it's hard to eat. Lorenzo is a budding percussionist and loves the snare drum. He is currently sporting a pair of 'Urkel' glasses, because he thought it would be kind of cool. Everybody at Diego is wearing these now—he kind of started a trend. *Diego, Ms. Ragus's sixth grade*

MELINDA HERNANDEZ was born with six fingers on each hand, though she doesn't have the extra fingers anymore. She likes playing rock songs on the electric guitar and her guitar group once played at the House of Blues. Friends would describe her as smart, funny, and goofy. *Diego, Ms. Alexandroff's sixth grade*

LUCERO HERRERA has one brother and two turtles. He has played the violin and the piano for three years. Lucero's mom thinks he should be a nurse because he is caring. *Mitchell, Mr. Woodland's fifth grade*

CHINA HILL loves to read and write—especially mystery or vampire stories. She wants to be a writer when she gets older. *Harvard, Ms. Hemesath's eighth grade*

ANTHONY HUERTA loves making art projects like 3D sculptures. He once found a toy dragon and painted it until it started to look so good he made it a showcase piece. It's a finished piece of artwork that he's proud of. *Mitchell, Ms. Riefenberg's fourth grade*

AATIANA HUNTER has two brothers, one sister, one cat, and no dogs. *Randolph, Ms. Moore's third grade*

GABRIEL HURTADO is a seven-year-old whose secret talent is basketball—he's been keeping this secret for a long time. He's more or less as good as Carlos Boozer. Gabriel would like to be an author when he grows up and write fiction stories about aliens and outer space. *Pulaski, Mrs. Navarro's second grade*

JILLIAN HUTTON has been taking Irish dance for as long as she can remember. The steps are cool and you get to have beautiful posture and neat hard and soft shoes. Jillian loves experimenting with art and making stuff with clay and fabric. *Pritzker, sixth grade, 826CHI tutoring*

ISMAEL IRIZARRY once went to Orlando, Florida, and thinks Sea World is cool! He is good at swimming and baseball (but not very good at football). Ismael thinks "tidbit" is a funny word. *Burr, Ms. Bergeson's third grade*

TAYLOR JACKSON loves to play football and loves to sing. *Diego, Ms. Alexandroff's sixth grade*

STORM JACKSON likes to read the Junie B. Jones books, along with other chapter and nonfiction books. She also likes playing jump rope with her little sister. Storm likes learning because, as she says, "if you want to know something or tutor someone or be a teacher, you have to know something yourself." *Randolph, Ms. Moore's third grade*

JUSTIN JEFFERSON is a great writer with a lot of imagination. *Randolph, Ms. Moore's third grade*

ANJELINA JOLEEN JIMENEZ once went to Mexico for her cousin's Communion. She would like to be a clothes designer. *Mitchell, Ms. Riefenberg's fourth grade*

JUSTIN JOHNSON has a really great Mohawk. He loves playing his PlayStation—maybe even a little too much. Justin is the funniest kid in school, as well as an honor student, and cornbread is his favorite food. *Drake, Mr. Coppola's eighth grade*

LEE KENDRICK has a younger brother who is five. Tamales are his favorite thing to eat because they are delicious and scrumptious. Lee plans to be an astronaut when he grows up. *Pulaski, Mrs. Shane's second grade*

DERRELL KILLINGSWORTH is a fun-loving person who loves to be outside and hang out with his friends. *Diego, Ms. Zavala's sixth grade*

ROXOLANA KRONSHTAL can read upside down. She is a mad artist—"like, all forms." When she grows up, Roxolana would like to be a chef or a lawyer. *Mitchell, Ms. Riefenberg's fourth grade*

DIANA LOPEZ likes to take walks in the rain and likes to match clothes. She is a huge animal lover and she loves to read romance novels. *Peabody, Mr. Simpson's seventh grade*

JAVON MACKEY took an interest in the guitar at the age of eleven. After two months of practice with instructor Professor Goldberg, Javon had his first recital at VanderCook College of Music. *Drake, Mr. Coppola's eighth grade*

JOWAN MACON says his friends are funny which causes him to be funny. Before Jowan writes, he always dances. *Harvard, Ms. Hemesath's eighth grade*

MARTA MARCZUK has never tried Brussels sprouts, but she doesn't think she is missing anything. Marta is a ballroom dancer and would like to be a scientist when she grows up. *Belding, Mrs. Nelson's seventh grade*

KIMBERLY MARTINEZ has played violin since the third grade. She also enjoys playing Zumba on her Nintendo Wii. *Mitchell, Mr. Woodland's fifth grade*

SARA MCDUFFORD is an artist who favors drawing aliens, horses, dragons, pigs, koalas, hawks, falcons, cardinals, any other kind of bird, pigs, unicorns, Komodo dragons, and dogs. Sara also likes to go to her aunt's house in Crystal Lake because they have dogs there. *LaSalle II, third grade, 826CHI tutoring*

BRITTANY MCPHERSON uses writing as a way to express herself. "When I start to write," says Brittany, "I get lost." Brittany works to put herself into her stories and to let readers get to understand her better as a person and as a writer. *Peabody, Mr. Simpson's seventh grade*

ANGELINE MEDINA has never met anyone else with her name. When she grows up, she plans to be a photographer and take pictures of people and plants. Angeline's favorite color is aquamarine. *Mitchell, Ms. Riefenberg's fourth grade*

MARC ANTHONY MENDEZ would like to have a secret invention like the characters in this book. Marc's favorite part of the day is when he makes a touchdown. *Pulaski, Mrs. Shane's second grade*

JONATHON ANGEL MERCADO has two brothers and one sister, and his family is Puerto Rican. He loves basketball and also plays the tenor saxophone. Jonathon would like to achieve all his goals in life. *Diego, Ms. Zavala's sixth grade*

OMAR MIRANDA likes to watch television with his dad. Someday, he plans be a famous soccer player for the Spanish national team. Omar practices playing soccer with his cousin on the weekends. *Pulaski, Ms. Meza's second grade*

KARINA MORALES likes singing, especially Selena Gomez songs. She wishes she could take a trip to Paris. People say Karina has an overactive imagination—which is a great thing for a writer! *Diego, Ms. Alexandroff's sixth grade*

LUCY NASH doesn't write a lot, but when she does, she really likes it. When she grows up, Lucy wants to be a dancer. She's still figuring out which kind. *Burr, Ms. Bergeson's third grade*

LIO NUNEZ really likes math and he's pretty good at it. Lio reads thirty minutes of facts every night before bed. *Belding, Mrs. Nelson's seventh grade*

MINA NUNEZ likes to draw anime characters, especially Naruto. When she is not drawing, she likes to play with her red-nosed Pit Bull named Mocha. Mina enjoys music and she plays the alto saxophone and the recorder. *Diego, Ms. Zavala's sixth grade*

NIFEMI OLUGBEMIGA taps her foot habitually when she knows she is going to sing. She loves to dance, but only in her room. *Peabody, Mr. Simpson's seventh grade*

AMYAH ORTEGA is very curious about books. She also loves painting flowers and fire. Actually, Amyah likes to draw pretty much anything—mostly at night when everyone is sleeping. *Pulaski, Mrs. Shane's second grade*

AYLIN ORTEGA is the only one she knows with her name, which is a traditional Mexican name. Aylin learned to read when she was three years old and her first book was *The Cat in the Hat. Tonti, Mrs. Kadow's fourth grade*

JOEL ORTIZ loves to be a Mexican-American and loves his family and friends. He also really likes music and technology. His favorite music is rap and he loves video games, like "NBA 2Kll"! *Tonti, Mrs. Kadow's fourth grade*

TYLER OSBEY likes it when things are clean and organized. He keeps his room clean by making sure to lock his door so his four-year-old sister can't get in and make a mess of his toys. When Tyler grows up, he wants to do what his dad does, which is to construct buildings. *Pulaski, Mrs. Shane's second grade*

JAVIER PACHECO has cousins in Puerto Rico. He's never met them, but one day, probably over summer break, he'd like to visit them. *Erie, Ms. DeVooght's fourth grade*

ANDRENIQUE PATTERSON loves to make up a story. Andrenique has eight sisters and brothers altogether—not counting her best friend Natasha, who is like another sister to her. They all love school and help out at home. *Randolph, Ms. Lohitsa's sixth grade*

ALEJANDRO PEREZ likes to play soccer and also likes Mexico. When Alejandro grows up, he wants to be a paleontologist. *Tonti, Mrs. Dussias-Cuevas's third grade*

IVAN PEREZ plays midfield and forward on his soccer team and scores a lot of goals. Someday, Ivan would like to play with Portuguese soccer star Cristiano Ronaldo. *Mitchell, Mr. Woodland's fifth grade*

ZOLA A. PRICE has written many songs about her dog George, who is a puggle. Zola also has a slight fear of clowns, also know as coulrophobia. *Home-schooled, sixth grade, 826CHI workshop*

ADRIAN QUINTERO enjoys spending time with her big brother and little sister and their new puppy, Principle. Adrian's mother is a doctor who helps her with her schoolwork at home and wants Adrian to go all the way to college. *Locke, Ms. Ruiz's third grade*

CATHLEEN RAMIREZ has one sister and one brother. They make her really happy. *Locke, Mrs. Alcantar's third grade*

CYNTHIA RAUDALES-ZAVALA says that swimming is her favorite activity. When she's not swimming, Cynthia likes to watch The Powerpuff Girls—she especially likes the character Bubble because she is so sweet. *Locke, Ms. Ruiz's third grade*

DASHYONNIA REDMOND loves to text all day and everyday. She estimates that she must send at least 100 a day. When Dashyonnia grows up, she's considering being a lawyer, a marriage counselor, and a writer. *Harvard, Ms. Hemesath's eighth grade*

ALIEZA RENTERIA is nine years old and feels lucky to have such wonderful parents. Alieza's mom cooks delicious foods and her dad always helps her with her homework. *Mitchell, Ms. Riefenberg's fourth grade*

JENNIFER RESENDIZ loves to play soccer and write funny stories. Some of Jennifer's stories are from the point-of-view of her beloved cat, Simba. *Burr, Mr. Patiño's fifth grade*

JAMELL RICHARDSON likes to eat French fries for breakfast and ice cream for lunch and dinner. Jamell also enjoys watching Power Rangers because they have a lot of cool inventions. *Pulaski, Mrs. Shane's second grade*

KRISTINE MARISOL RIOS has four brothers. When she grows up, Kristine wants to be a famous writer who also plays the saxophone. *Diego, Ms. Zavala's sixth grade*

MAJA RIVERA is in training for a dark blue belt in karate. Maja's family is originally from Malta, an island in Europe. *Burr, Ms. Bergeson's third grade*

ALMA RODRIGUEZ has been to Las Vegas when she was moving from Mexico, where she was born, to Chicago. Alma has also been to L.A. to visit family and she loves the beaches. *Burr, Mr. Patiño's fifth grade*

ANGEL ROJAS has a Pit Bull named Roc. She loves him a lot. *Tonti, Mrs. Dussias-Cuevas's third grade*

KAITLYN ROMO has a big sister who plays with her in the park. Her favorite food is chicken nuggets from anywhere. *Burr, Ms. Bergeson's third grade*

NANCY RUIZ likes to skateboard and her favorite trick is an ollie. She thinks it's pretty funny to run into things. Nancy also loves climbing trees to get to high places. *Diego, Ms. Zavala's sixth grade*

LESLIE D. SADKOWSKI once went to Poland to meet her distant family. When she grows up, Leslie would like to be a news reporter. *Mitchell, Ms. Riefenberg's fourth grade*

ARIANA SALGADO has visited Houston, Texas, when she went to see some of her family. Her favorite book is about bees and how they grow. It's called *Bees. Pulaski, Mrs. Shane's second grade*

BRIAN SAUCEDO likes to draw—sometimes he draws superheroes but lately he's drawing zombies. He is still working on them. *Tonti, Mrs. Kadow's fourth grade*

TAMIA SMITH has always wanted a turtle because they can't escape and because "turtle" starts with "T" like Tamia. Her favorite snack is cheese. Tamia loves to cook tacos, and she knows how to. *Randolph, Ms. Moore's third grade*

JENNIFER SORIA plays defense on her soccer team, the Golden Eagles. She thinks it's really cool that her aunt and uncle own a technology store. *Tonti, Mrs. Kadow's fourth grade*

CHEROKEE SPERRY loves fried chicken and candy apples. He is also a novice hunter. *St. Ferdinand, sixth grade, 826CHI workshop*

PENELOPE SYMONDS likes doing arts and crafts like crocheting and drawing. Penelope is allergic to cats, but she has two rabbits, a dog, a bird, and two fish. *Belding, Mrs. Nelson's seventh grade*

ROCKIA TAYLOR loves writing and her favorite book is *Myself and I.* Rockia would like you to know that Ms. Hemesath is the best reading and writing teacher ever. *Harvard, Ms. Hemesath's eighth grade*

BELICIA VEGA loves to swim and dance and play tag with her cat, whose name is Prince Wolffy. Someday, Belicia would like to work in a pet store feeding the animals. *Pulaski, Mrs. Shane's second grade*

HILDA VILLA likes to sing songs by Lady Gaga. Her family is from Durango, Mexico, and she thinks it is beautiful there. At home, Hilda helps cook tamales, tacos, and enchiladas. *Mitchell, Mr. Woodland's fifth grade*

EMONI WALKER is really good at writing paragraphs. She would love to visit California one day. *Randolph, Ms. Moore's third grade*

AUDRIANNA WALLER likes drawing and painting faces and cities, and art is her favorite hobby. She also does hip hop, ballroom dance, and cheerleading. When she's not busy with these activities, Audrianna likes to play tag with her sisters. *Drake, Mrs. Bowen's fourth grade*

GRACE WHITESIDE has one sister, one dog, four cats, and a hamster. She loves to do gymnastics. *Burr, Ms. Bergeson's third grade*

SOPHIA WILLIAMS has two dogs and one little sister. In her spare time, Sophia likes to tumble. *Bell, sixth grade, 826CHI workshop*

DONTE WILLIAMS was born in Illinois on the East Side. Donte has never had bad grades, and he is currently working hard and trying to get in a good high school. *Harvard, Ms. Hemesath's eighth grade*

BRYAN WILLIAMS is good at running. Bryan's favorite sport is football, and he loves tacos. *Drake, Mrs. Bowen's fourth grade*

JAEDEN WRIGHT wants to be a teacher when he grows up so that he can help kids get a head start on going to college. *Randolph, Ms. Moore's third grade*

OUR CONTRIBUTORS

A. Philip Randolph Elementary School

MS. LOHITSA'S SIXTH GRADE CLASS

Aaron Armstrong	Shakiyah Asphy	Brandon Barner
Devenus Borders	Demetrius Borders	Diamond Braxton
Labrenda Dobbs	Jaquise Evans	Christopher Ferguson
Malika Holman	Heaven Ingram	Semaj Lawshea
Jalen Mckinney	Montana Meyers	Chad Mims
Erica Morgan	Terrence Nelson	Infinity Palmer
Andrenique Patterson	Natasha Pearson	Taicheal Petty
Jillian Rupert	Ebony White	Nehemiah Thomas
Jazmyne Williams-Anderson		

MS. MOORE'S THIRD GRADE CLASS

Khenede Allen	Jakyah Amous	Jada Bell
Jazmine Bell	Osmond Bell, Jr.	Malachi Catchings
Porsha Donner	Kameron Duncan	Donisha Ephraim
Marissa Glenn	Mariyah Green	Marktwain Green
Aatiana Hunter	Storm Jackson	Justin Jefferson
Maki Johnson	Fontane Lewis	Donovan Luckett
Aaliyah Mcgruder	Jeremy Mitchell	Jonathan Riley, Jr.
Jona Rogers	Brandion Smith	Kelise Smith
Tamia Smith	Mykayla Spires	Emoni Walker
Imoni Walker	Anthony Williams	Dorian Woods
Jaeden Wright		

Elizabeth P. Peabody School

MR. SIMPSON'S SEVENTH GRADE CLASS

Larone Brim, Jr.	Malik Brown	Johana Castelan
Jenesse David	Dimitri Deangelo	Ismael Garcia
Kimberly Gutierrez	Ayreial Harris	Ariana Hernandez
Atanacio Hernandez	Ramon Hernandez	Katara Jackson
Diana Lopez	Brittany McPherson	Juan Munoz
Martin Munoz	Esmeralda Olivier	Oluwanifemi Olubemiga

Yarett Parada
Marlon Salgado
Billy Washington

Jose Penaloza
Alexis Serrato
Briana Winters

Carolina Rodriguez
Horacio Soto

Ellen Mitchell Elementary School

MS. RIEFENBERG'S FOURTH GRADE CLASS

Natalie Alicea
Victoria Cortez
Anthony Huerta
Paul Koroluk
Joshua Moreno
Julian Pacalso
Alieza Renteria
Ruben Romo
Jonathan Torres
Deandre Watson

Gregory Birge
Carlos Diaz
Anjelina Joleen Jimenez
Roxolana Kronshtal
Tashawn Morris
Marlen Patino
Natty Rodriguez
Leslie D. Sadkowski
Clifton Turner

Alexander Calvo
Emily Gonzalez
Marqious Johnson
Angeline Medina
Armani Osorio
Dominic Principato
Jeremiah Roman
Rosie Talavera
Isaiah Ward

MR. WOODLAND'S FIFTH GRADE CLASS

Alejandro Arellano
Cindy Bahena
Josue Barreiro
James Brock
Kiara Diaz
Melissa Gomez
Imari Herrera
Pablo Martinez
Joshua Ortiz
Ivan Perez
David Rivera
Priscilla Trinidad

Selina Arroyo
Kimberly Bañuelos
Amaria Birge
Alex Campos
Jiovanni Fernandez
Enrique Hernandez
Lucero Herrera
Eduardo Medina
Kasandra Paredes
Azalia Resendiz
Emily Salgado
Nakiya Turner

Emily Avila
Claudia Barreiro
Jovan Bradley
David Carnalla
Rey Flores
Erick Hernandez
Kimberly Martinez
Jose Medina
Mario Pena
Evan Reynolds
Ziggy Sandifer
Hilda Villa

Enrico Tonti Elementary School

MRS. DUSSIAS-CUEVAS'S THIRD GRADE CLASS

Sophia Aguilera
Andrew Ayala

Aylin Aguilar
Miriam Becerra

Baby Antunez
Damitres Boyd

Barbara Gamez
Mahogani Johnson
Leilani Martinez
Mario Nunez
Kenneth Ortiz
Serena Quinones
Angel Rojas
Victor Torres

Gabriella Guillen
Fernando Lara
Michael Master
Fatima Oivares
Leonardo Palomar
Lizbeth Ramirez
Enrique Sanchezlara
Jacqueline Vega

Quincy Holmes
Moises Lopez
Luis Mora
Jefferson Olivera
Alejandro Perez
Jonathon Rivera
Jose Tapia
Deontie Wormley

MRS. KADOW'S FIFTH GRADE CLASS

Jasmine Alamilla
Janette Avalos
Manuel Guzman
Heidi Hernandez
Roberto Liberato
Miroslava Martinez
Gonzalo Ortega
Samantha Poorman
Jonathan Santoyo
Jennifer Soria
Karissa Urbina

Alma Andrade
Kyle Calvin
Lealanie Gutierrez
Marilu Herrera
Deyanira Lopez
Dioceline Miranda
Joel Ortiz
Stephanie Romano
Brian Saucedo
Humberto Torres

Ezequiel Aranda
Samantha Campos
Sesash Gutierrez
Oscar Isidoro
Rosario Martinez
Aylin Ortega
John Pedroza
Alexis Sanchez
Nancy Saucedo
Liliana Trevino

Erie Elementary Charter School

MS. DEVOOGHT'S FOURTH GRADE CLASS

Maxim Andriychuk
Taylor Brown
Jireh Kelsey
Gizelle Marino
Elizabeth Orta
Hazel Pagaza
Donovan Smith

Jennifer Arreola
Melanie Candelario
Sierra Lewis
Ashley Martinez
Christian Ortiz
Valente Renteria
Jocilyn Vazquez

Joi Bradley
Jamilet Garcia
Mia Loeffler-Martinez
Alexis Mendez
Javier Pacheco
Kenneth Sanchez
Fatima Weiner

MR. MITCHELL'S FOURTH GRADE CLASS

Maria Isabel Allen Cardona
Alicia Collazo
Ethan Corona
Hunter Dotzert

Mia Baez-Vasquez
Edgar Contreras
Abril Cruz
Mikalah Dunbar

Lamiyah Boyce
Lee Jahia Cook
Divine Davenport
Jennifer Garcia

Saul Garcia

Emily Mancilla

Samanta Reyes

Ritley Vasquez

Elizabeth Hernandez

Adrian Martinez

Elijah Roman

Isabell Zavala

Amanda Jones

Khaimen Ramirez-Ross

Hannia Valera

John B. Drake Elementary School

MRS. BOWEN'S FOURTH GRADE CLASS

Chiquita Baptiste

Jonay Brown

Tamaran Duncan

Nicholas Goodloe

Diovione Harris

Najee Jackson

Destiny Lloyd

Nauledge Mcnear

Miracle Pinkston

Dora Sarpong

Bryan Williams

Safire Baptiste

Jannie Counts

Johnny Evans, Jr.

Niguel Gordon

Lazara Harrison

Raheem Johnson, Jr.

Laveata Lowe

Maurionna Minor

Gregory Profit, Jr.

Audrianna Waller

Imanni Brittman

Tamara Duncan

Andres Gonzalez

Allyea Harris

Steven Hawthorne

Kayla Lewis

Trinity Loyd

Ladarrion Moore

Diamond Rencher

Aniaah Washington

MR. COPPOLA'S EIGHTH GRADE CLASS

Dejuan Banks

Breanna Blocker

Jazmine Brown

Nia Gipson

Disante Hayes

Justin Johnson

Javon Mackey

Lavarius Moore

Javier Richardson

Deshawn Banks

Essence Brown

Alonzo Cozart

Kenyhatta Goggins

Daijah Jackson

Trelah Jordan

Robert Montgomery

Narketa Pickett

Benjamin Waters

Camerion Blair

Jason Brown

Alexis Gibson

Deondre Hall

Henry Jackson

Tiana Lweis

Jejuan Moore

Sylvester Ratcliffe

Moesha Winston

Harvard School Of Excellence

MS. HEMESATH'S EIGHTH GRADE GIRLS CLASS

Keyshawna Beard

LaKayla Bradley

Mashaya Covington

Shania Bell

Jamaiya Cohen

Essence Frieson

Samone Boone

Pricilla Concepcion

China Hill

Chevette Johnson
Alexis Malone
Jessica Peake
Myesha Riddle
Narkesha Smith
Monesha Williams
Rockia Taylor

Gabriella Lacy
Kaylan Moore
Dashyonnia Redmond
Nataysia Rush
Antonisha Spencer
Royeshia Williams

Blaire Lovette
Darian Payton
LaRhonda Reed
Shalamiyah Salter
LaQuita Weatherspoon
Kamiya Wilson

MS. HEMESATH'S EIGHTH GRADE BOYS CLASS

Clifton Black
Martez Crosby
Shondell Hughes
Cornelius Nunn
Lorenzo Riley
Marlin Scott
Malik Thompson

John Cain
Christopher Dampier
Jowan Macon
Austin Portis
Tyray Roberson
Ryan Smith
Christian Washington

French Cribbs
Ramel Greene
Alonzo Moore
Michael Riddle
Lamont Smith
Diamontae Swan
Donte Williams

Hiram H. Belding Elementary School

MRS. NELSON'S SEVENTH GRADE CLASS—PERIOD ONE

Giovanni Arroyo
Dion Valention Benson
Zakaria Chihab
Cynthia Gallegos
David Richard Lemus
Geodonna Catherine Matthews
Amanda Moore
Olga E. Pilch
Reham Ali Khan Sabarna
Maria Tinajero

Emily Barraza
Diana Karmina Bustamante
Cesar Fernandez
Arnel Karaduz
Imane Mahmahi
Jose Medrano
Lio Nunez
Julianno Jesus Pujols
Hajira Sultana
Ruben Edurado Valdez

Loreyn R. Benigno
Sadie Castro
Justine Fugate
Rhita Koubbi
Marta Marczuk
Fardosa Mohamed
Erik Arnoldo Olivares
Maria Guadalupe Quinones
Nathaniel Isaac Taggart

MRS. NELSON'S SEVENTH GRADE CLASS—PERIOD TWO

Amine Ahmedyahia
Abed Jalil Atiyeh
Michael A.Demasy
Audrey Jubilee Hernandez
Sade Alicia Madrigal

Christon Joe Allam
Walid Bouchama
Steven Figueroa
Grace Kozisek
Carlos Israel Martinez

Grace Isabelle Andre
Destiny Julissa Coffman
Carlos Daniel Garcia
Jordan Alexander Lozinski
Donna Julissa Ortega

Evangelina Pacheco
Yasmine Latae Redeaux
Ahlam Salman
Gloria Beth Vogt

Juan Miguel Perez
Abigail Renteria
Penelope Symonds

Alexander Popov
Dylan Riedy
Michelle Jennifer Vega

Jonathan Burr Elementary School

MS. BERGESON'S THIRD GRADE CLASS

Victor Bustamante
Catherine Galvan
Ismael Irizarry
Isaiah Montoya
Brianna Quiroz
Ilean Snodie
Melony Vizcarra

Isaac Espiritu
Jazmin Gonzalez
Hisham Kysia
Lucy Nash
Maja Rivera
Areli Velazquez
Grace Whiteside

Ayliehla Fairfax
Marisol Guerrero
Andrew MacPhetres
Ashantae Pillman
Kaitlyn Romo
Kassandra Virola

MR. PATIÑO'S FIFTH GRADE CLASS

Makayla Bradford
Nain Galo
Starr Kujawamahnesmith
Diana Mendez
Diego Peralta
Korshicia Richardson
Vanessa Roldan
Mikael Simmons
Savannah Vasquez

Salvador Bustamante
Marvin Galvan
Ariasne Marquez
Jared Monarrez
Leenishia Pettigrew
Isabel Rocha
Yuribeth Salgado
Alexis Stephens
Rafael Vazquez

Josian Cruz
Emily Hernandez
Genesis McCullum
Bryan Montalban
Jennifer Resendiz
Alma Rodriguez
Arani Shearill
Priscilla Vargas
Alisette Virola

José De Diego Community Academy

MS. ALEXANDROFF'S SIXTH GRADE CLASS

Jorge Abreu
Esteban Caro
Keila Estrada
Melinda Hernandez
Liana Lorenzi
Monica Martinez
Esmeralda Miranda

Esmeralda Arroyo
Seth Corpuz
Brian Frometa
Eliza Hoyos
Kalyani Maldonado
Mya McKennie
Karina Morales

Emily Bermudez
Keisha Diaz
Gialisse Garcia
Taylor Jackson
Jaylen Martinez
Jose Melecio
Gabriel Munoz

Javier Munoz
Esteban Ramos
Jose Romero
Leilani Vellon

Amanda Navarro
Kiara Rodriguez
Ibrahim Sabbi
Kavaris Wilson

Maria Orduño
Rebekah Rodriguez
Niacole Vazquez

MS. RASGUS'S SIXTH GRADE CLASS

Kalen Aaron
Jasmine Burns
Lorenzo Harris
Barbara Jimenez-Soriano
Jordan Melendez
Marvin Ochoa
Secily Pinero
Carlos Roldan
Lucero Sandoval
Nallely Silva
Leslie Torres

Coby Akins
Hector Crespo
Kiara Hernandez
Guillermo Lopez
Jomaris Mercado
Elliseo Ortiz
Jocelyn Rivera
Taina Salinas
Estefania Santiago
Wilfredo Silva

Armando Arismendis
Lexi Del Toro
Kendall Hull
Jose Martinez
Jorge Miranda
Nathaniel Perez
Xavier Rivera
Arely Sanchez
Luis Serrano
Matthew Tanon

MS. ZAVALA'S SIXTH GRADE CLASS

Jovan Alduen
Katherine Brito
Harry Gandia
Elisabel LaTorre
Yezenia Meraz
Mariah Munoz
Mina Nunez
Jennifer Perez
Kristine Marisol Rios
Carlos Rodriguez
Brianna Santiago

Christian Barcenas
Maicol Cabrera
Derrell Killingsworth
Mary Lutz
Jonathan Angel Mercado
Jared Navarro
Anthony Otero
Gaspar Rios
Chasity Rivera
Victoria Rodriguez
Jose Santiago

Isaias Berrios
Aaron Concepcion
Lazeric Lang
Ariel Menendez
Marlena Mendez
Jeremiah Navarro
Jilliann Paloma
Katherine Rios
Luis Rivera
Nancy Ruiz

Josephine Locke Elementary School

MRS. ALCANTAR'S THIRD GRADE CLASS

Emily Alvarado
Jose Castillo
Eduardo Delgado

Andrea Calderon
Alondra Chavez
Kevin Delgado

Dasyi Calderon
Axel Cruz
Ana Flores

Claudia Garcia
Alexa Herrera
Guadalupe Jaimes
Stephanie Quinones
Ashley Razo
Omar Sanchez
Nereida Villalobos

Anahy Gonzalez
Christian Honorato
Patty Lopez
Cathleen Ramirez
Christopher Rodriguez
Ashley Torres
Cristal Zenon

Yahir Hernandez
Andrea Ildefonso
Esmeralda Nunez
Karime Ramirez
Cristopher Rodriguez
Cynthia Uribe

MS. RUIZ'S THIRD GRADE CLASS

Jayson Agsalud
Stephanie Andrade
Yasmin Beltran
Ehab Dahbour
Edgar Gabriel
Alma Gonzalez
Miguel Madrigal
Kimberly Ramirez
Alejandro Silva

Cristian Aguirre
Fatima Anguiano
Isaac Bernal
Nykita Dirkans
Gustavo Gabriel
Jose Hernandez
Johnny Martinez
Cynthia Raudales-Zavala
Ronald Uruchima

James Andersen III
David Banacki
Jazlyn Crespo
David Dunbar
Natalie Garza
Rebecca Hernandez
Adrian Quintero
Sergio Rodriguez

Pulaski International School Of Chicago

MS. MEZA'S SECOND GRADE CLASS

Christopher Armijo
Christian Banuelos
Daniel Cruz
Christopher Dorantes
Alexis Garcia-Sanchez
Raul Herrera
Emanuel Mendoza
Luis Morales
Kevin Sanchez

Angelica Arroyo
Yadhira Bernal
Mario De La Torre
Jason Feliciano
Yair Gonzalez
Cesar Lopez
Daphne Meza
Katya A Ramirez

Kenya Bahena
Valery Castillo
Jose David Delgado
Berenice Flores
Cristopher Guiracocha
Sergio Mendieta
Omar Miranda
Uriel Rodriguez

MRS. SHANE'S SECOND GRADE CLASS

Gabriel Andaluz
Eva Bernatek
Jadalynne Gago-Izquierdo
Angel Guerrero

Jason Aviles
Yahir Flores
Angel Garcia
Jocelyn Herrera

Princess Ballog
Carly Freeman
Christian Garcia
Lee Kendrick

Marc Anthony Mendez
Tyler Osbey
Justin Rodriguez
Diana Vazquez
Julissa Villalobos

Jovani Montanez
Mellanie Palacios
Ariana Salgado
Belicia Vega

Amyah Ortega
Jamell Richardson
Sofia Salgado
Richard Velasco

MRS. NAVARRO'S SECOND GRADE CLASS

Kevin Arias
Jorge Cebrero
Jose Chavez
Grace Heredia
Jaime Marchan
David Mejia
Sandra Ordas
Adam Reyes
Angelica Santoyo
Ivar Wolf

Ashley Arroyo
Alma Ceron
Viviana De Alba
Diana Hernandez
Citlalli Marquez
Stephanie Morales
Adrian Ramirez
Julius Salas
Erica Vargas

Jordi Castro
Delilah Chavez
Elizabeth De Leon
Gabriel Hurtado
Daniela Martinez
Hikari Nakasone
Jared Renteria
Alexis Santiago
Fernando Vargas

Contributors From 826CHI's Workshops Program

Brennen Bariso
Jack Herbst
Quinn Mankowski
Zola A. Price
Cherokee Sperry

Sarah Breinig
Zoe Kane
Lucille McKnight
Jennifer Resendiz
Alisette Virola

Michelle Cardona
Courtney Mankowski
Alec Perez
Scott Skiba
Sophia Williams

Contributors From 826CHI's After-School Tutoring And Writing Program

Jasmine Aguilar
Ivanova Alaniz
Michelle Cardona
Catherine Galvan
Jalina Garay
Jillian Hutton
Thayss Lopez
Kaleb Melendez
Brian Montalban
Jocelyn Ortega
Phillip Ramey
Kaitlyn Romo
Emma Santiago
Tania Soto
Gabriel Villalva
Ella Watson

Oscar Aguilar
Lauren Alaniz
DeAndre Durham
Kimberly Galvan
Justina Garriga
Carlos Jimenez
Sara McDufford
Jared Monarrez
Evelyn Montalban
Amalia Pappa
Jennifer Resendiz
Karina Romo
Kayla Santiago
Sabrina Suchecka
Alisette Virola

Jonathan Akins
Dionne Beals
Anthony Fernandez
Marvin Galvan
Mikey Hicks
Juan Jimenez
Anjel Melendez
Aliha Montalban
Axel Ortega
Leenishia Pettigrew
Cristian Rodriguez
Nalani Sandoval
Scott Skiba
Sebastian Suchecki
Kassandra Virola

ACKNOWLEDGEMENTS

Like all that we do at 826CHI, this book would not have been possible without the extraordinary talents and inspiring commitment of our volunteers and Board of Directors. Their boundless enthusiasm and wholehearted belief in the power of student writing is behind each and every story in this book. We know that many of these stories took shape because of the remarkable vision and thoughtful urging of the following volunteers: Aaron Adler, Hassan Ali, Leah Allen, Matt Anglen, Rachel Angres, Erik Barragan, Shanita Bigelow, Suzy Broz, Brad Brubaker, Debbie Capone, Andres Carrasquillo, Carrie Colpitts, Jeni Crone, Lindsay Davis, Theresa Duffy, Manal Farhan, Rachel Fields, Adam Findlay, Alice Foreman, Jenny Gillespie, Jess Gordan, Justin Gumiran, Seth Herr, Brenna Ivey, Lara Kattan, Jean Khut, Jamie Knight, Josh Lesser, Tricia Lunt, Colleen Malone, Victoria McManus, Eric Miller, Hayley Miller, Beth Osborn, Laura Perelman, Sarah Polen, Janet Potter, Megan Ryan, Meggen Saka, Anthony Shaker, Jordan Shappell, Jessica Sime, Dana Stewart, Diana Tang, and Kara Thorstenson. To each of these outstanding individuals we send our profound thanks for joining us on this particular adventure.

We offer special thanks to volunteer Aparna Puppula, who lived this book for weeks on end, leading many of the publication's projects in schools around the city, and offering careful feedback throughout the process. Aparna, the way we you feel about Ophelia is the way we feel about you, and we could not be more grateful for the many ways in which you helped make this book a reality.

Also instrumental in this project were 826CHI interns Saarah

Malik and Colin Packard, who typed up approximately two billion pages of student writing over the course of the project, helped with countless organizational tasks in assembling the book, and brought their phenomenal energy into classroom after classroom. If "Master Tidbits" ever goes to Broadway, you will definitely be the stars.

This book was made a reality through the invaluable generosity of one anonymous donor. We can never adequately express our gratitude for the opportunity you have given our students, both to become published authors and to share their amazing stories with the public. Most great stories have at least one hero, a knight in shining armor—or, in very rare cases, an intrepid lizard-scientist— and in this story you are certainly ours. Your unbelievable kindness will be remembered always, as it continues to inspire these students and others for years to come. Thank you.

For his tireless work and epic creativity, we thank Thomas Quinn, graphic designer extraordinaire. His ability to seamlessly unite the words of so many students within a single work was nothing short of astounding, and we are grateful for the countless hours he devoted to doing so. For their proofreading expertise, we are also grateful to Lori Barrett, Emily Buckler, and Staci Davidson, who somehow manage to make spell checking exceptionally fun.

If we were better artists, we'd draw several graphic novels to represent our gratitude to cartoonists Aaron Renier and Laura Park. They would be superheroes in every panel. Alas, we are not exceptional artists, but we are so very glad that they are, and glad also for the way they took the unique visions of each and every student and sketched out something amazing. When we asked

Aaron to do ten drawings for the book, he asked us if he and Laura could do a hundred. We are still awestruck by this conversation, and even more so by the incredible artwork it elicited.

Finally, we offer our heartfelt thanks to the many teachers and administrators who collaborated with 826CHI throughout this project, taking time out of busy days to welcome volunteers into their classrooms to work with their students. We are grateful for all of their time and communication and also for the excitement they continue to share with us about their students' writing. We are grateful, above all, for the invaluable work they are doing each day.

Mara O'Brien, *Executive Director*
Kait Steele, *Director of Education and Publications*
Zach Duffy, *Director of Development*
Patrick Shaffner, *Outreach Director and Boring Store Head Spy*
Kendra Curry, *Program and Volunteer Coordinator*

On a similar note of thanks, we can't recommend the following websites highly enough:

Thomas Quinn — *Designer*
http://thomasjquinn.com

Aaron Renier — *Cartoonist*
http://aaronrenier.com

Laura Park — *Cartoonist*
http://www.singingbones.com

ABOUT 826CHI

826CHI is a non-profit organization dedicated to supporting students ages 6 to 18 with their creative and expository writing skills, and to helping teachers inspire their students to write. Our mission is based on the understanding that great leaps in learning can happen with one-on-one attention, and that strong writing skills are fundamental to future success.

826CHI provides after-school tutoring, class field trips, writing workshops, and in-schools programs—all free of charge—for students, classes, and schools. All of our programs are challenging and enjoyable, and ultimately strengthen each student's power to express ideas effectively, creatively, confidently, and in his or her individual voice.

Each year we serve four thousand students, something that would not be possible without the amazing commitment of our dedicated volunteers. These published authors, editors, professors, playwrights, journalists, artists, actors, and architects, to name a few, staff each and every program that 826CHI offers.

826CHI is one of eight chapters of 826 National, a non-profit tutoring, writing, and publishing organization with locations in eight cities across the country. 826 Valencia, the flagship center in San Francisco, was founded by writer/editor Dave Eggers and educator Nínive Calegari in 2002. 826CHI opened its doors to Chicago students in October of 2005, joining 826 Valencia, 826 LA, 826 NYC, 826 Seattle, and 826 Michigan. In 2007, 826 Boston joined our national network of 826 chapters. In 2010, we were excited to welcome 826 DC as the most recent addition to the 826 family.

Our Programs

826CHI's free programs reach students at every opportunity—in school, after school, in the evenings, and on weekends.

AFTER-SCHOOL TUTORING AND WRITING

826CHI's site is packed five afternoons a week with students who come in for free one-on-one tutoring after school. Students are welcome to show up any school day, Monday through Thursday, from 3:00 until 5:30 p.m., and high school students are welcome to our Saturday afternoon sessions, as well. We serve students of all skill levels and interests, most of whom live or go to school within walking distance of our writing center. Literacy and writing are stressed through daily reading and monthly chapbook projects, where students' writing around a particular theme is compiled into small books and shared at family and community readings.

FIELD TRIPS

We help teachers get their students excited about writing while also helping students better express their ideas. 826CHI invites teachers to bring their students to our site for high-energy field trips during the school days. Teachers choose from several field trip formats depending on their interests and grade level. Our most popular field trip is *Storytelling & Bookmaking*, during which students write, illustrate, and bind their own books within a two-hour period. The field trip program is so popular that our schedule is filled almost a year in advance.

IN-SCHOOLS

It is not feasible for all classes to come to us, so we regularly dispatch teams of volunteers into local schools. At a teacher's request, we will send tutors into classrooms around the city to provide one-on-one assistance to students as they tackle various projects, including bookmaking, research papers, literary magazines, basic writing assignments, and college entrance essays. Work through the in-schools program may be project-specific or long-term.

WORKSHOPS

826CHI offers free workshops that provide in-depth writing instruction in a variety of areas that schools often cannot include in their curriculum, such as journalism, comic book making, playwriting, and songwriting. Innovative workshops with offbeat topics allow students to hone and advance their skills while having fun and developing a greater sense of the joy of writing. All workshops are project-based and are taught by experienced, accomplished professionals and volunteers. Connecting Chicago students with these creative and generous mentors allows students to dream and achieve on a grand scale.

STUDENT PUBLISHING

At 826CHI, we know the quality of student work is greatly enhanced when it is shared with an authentic audience. All of our activities are project-based, whether they result in an end-of-project book, a class performance, a gallery exhibit, a short film, or an exceptionally rockin' CD. As a writing center, we are especially committed to publishing student work, whether it be in the form of small chapbooks that we bind in-house or in professionally published volumes, such as this one. All forms of student publishing are available for purchase at The Boring Store and on our website.

Please visit us online at www.826chi.org or in-person at 1331 N. Milwaukee Avenue in Chicago's Wicker Park neighborhood to learn more about our programs and to find out how you can get involved.

THE BORING STORE

To crack this coded message, you'll need to reflect upon what it's trying to tell you:

Psst! 826CHI shares its space with The Boring Store, Chicago's only undercover secret agent supply store. The Boring Store outfits its spy-entele with the latest and greatest in espionagical wares. All funds raised through sales in the store go to support 826CHI's free programming.

The Boring Store's brick and mortar shop is certainly the place to visit if you're in desperate need of a grappling hook, a book to read on a long stakeout, messenger pigeon feed, or a t-shirt. We encourage you to sneak on over at your stealthiest convenience. Can't risk being tailed by enemy agents? Have no fear. You can also conduct your espionage operations online at **www.notasecretagentstore.com.**